To Mrs. Adamson with
in appreciation for sup,
yeas.

Edwin & Dorothy Hyland

The Horses Knew the Way

THE HORSES
KNEW THE WAY

Memories of a Lincolnshire Life

Frank Moore and *John Hynam*

ALAN SUTTON

First published in the United Kingdom in 1991
Alan Sutton Publishing Ltd · Phoenix Mill · Far Thrupp · Stroud
Gloucestershire

First published in the United States of America in 1992
Alan Sutton Publishing Inc · Wolfeboro Falls · NH 03896-8840

British Library Cataloguing in Publication Data

Moore, Frank
The horses knew the way : memories of a
Lincolnshire life.
I. Title II. Hynam, John
942.53

ISBN 0-86299-989-8

Library of Congress Cataloging in Publication Data applied for

Typeset in Garamond 12/14
Typesetting and origination by
Alan Sutton Publishing Limited.
Printed in Great Britain by
Hartnolls Ltd., Bodmin.

Contents

CONTENTS

Ploughing

The soil is rich, and easy turned
All through the mighty fen,
And little do I need, to be
The happiest of men.

There's Punch and Blossom, Flower too,
We four have worked for years,
Through autumn, winter and the spring,
On to the golden ears.

Their tread is steady, light and sure,
The furrow curls away; three
Shining horses, brown and strong,
Who work the live-long day.

Three understanding creatures who
Accept me as their guide;
I must be worthy of their trust,
And always on their side.

This single line gives me command,
A word, a gentle touch,
I've got a reputation, here,
Though you mightn't think it much.

        I am all men to these good three,
        I'm all the human race,
        I hope that, in their secret minds
        I'll never fall from grace.

Punch and Flower and Blossom too,
We plod on day by day,
Believe me when I tell you that
The horses knew the way.

Preface

About Frank Moore: he is a thinnish, medium sort of man, with dark and slowly disappearing hair, and a close look around the eyes which comes, no doubt, from having spent the last fifty and more years sizing up man and beast and not being wrong very often. We talked and talked with the recorder reels slowly taking in my life as well as his. We were together in mind at the first meeting; country-born myself, I lived my own youth again, and it was a happy experience.

But there's no need to tell you much about him. You have only to look at the title which chose itself. In five words, that's Frank.

JOHN HYNAM
PETERBOROUGH
Spring, 1970

CHAPTER ONE

Beginning

In the summer of 1910 my dad worked on the farm at Hopethorpe. My four brothers did too, but I was the baby of the family and I still had to go to school. What were we like? I'll use a word not in fashion these days. We were respectable. We were brought up in the atmosphere of farming, and with the idea that 'farm comes first'.

My father was a biggish man, and not backward in coming forward when he felt that there was something wrong that ought to be righted. The wrongest thing we could do (which we never did) was to be unkind to an animal, particularly to a horse.

'If you're a man what looks after horses, then the horses come first.' That was what my father said, and he lived by his own rule. He had a special understanding of horses; in more enlightened times he would have been given a grant to train as a vet, because he was a natural. He had the hands. He always said that if you fed a horse right, and worked it right, then it should never be ill. A big statement, but everyone admitted that Arthur Moore's horses looked the best and worked the best, and they won whatever prizes were going. When they didn't win, it was a loss by a very narrow margin.

Many's the time people have sent for him, instead of the vet. You only sent for the vet in dire emergency, which meant in practice that you sent for him when Arthur Moore was not available. When they asked my father to come, they knew that the horse would get the fullest attention possible, and not so much for what they 'let him have' (in money), but because he was there, a man of the village, one of 'us' instead of one of 'them'. Father used to say that every single case he was asked to put his reputation at stake, but I can remember hearing it said; 'If Moore couldn't do anything for it, you'd ha' thrown your money away sending for the vet.' That made me feel very proud. Small wonder then that I should, in looking up to my father, look up to the beasts he tended, and with which he could at times be so close and private.

However, I didn't start work on the farm where my father worked. Until we moved into Lincolnshire, I wasn't a regular farmhand anyway. My first horses were the responsibility of the man who drove the station carriage, and took the lords and ladies up to the great hall. That made the driver of those horses an important man to me, and the horses he used were slimmer, faster-looking beasts. When I think back, I can see that they were really very ordinary nags, reasonably well cared for, but for me they had wings on their hooves and fires in their nostrils.

I let myself be exploited by the man who drove them, and I didn't care.

'Like to help with the horses, boy?'

'Oh yes sir, please!'

'Are yer a good polisher?'

'Polish anything sir!'

He took me into the harness room, and showed me round, gave me the horse's gear and some rags and polish, and I set to work. There are dangers in loving a job. All I ever got for my love was a piece of cake; he knew that I needed no bribe to set me working, that I'd work for nothing but the sheer pleasure of it. When he let me rub the horse down or put the gear on I felt on top of the world. My mother knew where I was, attendant at the court of one of the kings of beasts.

My father got to know; he always got to know. It seemed that truth and facts were just drawn to his transparent honesty.

'And what's he pay you, boy?'

I told him; we never lied to father.

'Bit o' cake?' exclaimed my father with deep scorn. 'And while you're slaving away at that harness he's feeding his face in the kitchen, along with the servant girls. Huh!' And my father glared at the table. This meant that he was put out with someone outside the family. If ever he was upset by one of the family he soon said who it was

Arthur (named after my father and nicknamed 'Trunkie') said to me later, 'Told you, didn't I? Dad don't like Bowers. Had a row with him. And farm foreman told him off; said he didn't look after the carriage horses properly.'

Trunkie was surprised when I burst into tears. Come to that, so was I. He was good, though; he didn't jeer. He just asked why. Then I said: 'What I've done's no good then, is it? I did my best to look after the carriage horses properly; I did my best, but that wa'n't good enough!'

I didn't go near Mr Bowers and his carriage horses again. There's no more disheartening thing than what I'd suffered, or thought I'd suffered. I was miserable, and it showed everywhere.

I tried to pull myself together after a couple of days, because I overheard my mother say that they'd better keep an eye on me, because she thought I was sickening for something. I was, but not the way she meant, and when I met Mr Bowers in the village street I turned and ran.

It was my father who put things right. 'Do you still want to work with the horses, Frank?'

'Yes please, Dad!'

He looked at me solemnly. 'Horses are important creatures, boy. They're sensible. I could name folks as would have to go hard at it to be as important as one or two horses we've got at the farm. Living creatures, with hearts and brains and strength. And every one's different from all the others. You've got to know 'em. So, we'll have it done the proper way. You come along o' me, and we'll start your education, eh?'

Suddenly the sun came out.

CHAPTER TWO

Salt on a Few Tails

In those days we were poor, but I reckon that farm workers today aren't really as well off as we were all those years ago. The thing I'm saying is, we didn't *feel* poor. We weren't short of food or clothes. We had the bread and sometimes the butter, and a little jam from time to time. Mother, who worked harder than Father, was a great one for altering and mending and making things do. I never once felt awkward or ashamed at wearing cut-downs of my brothers' clothes. From one point of view I liked it better. You see, we had our everyday clothes, and then a suit of 'Sundays'. Sunday *was* Sunday, no error. We all went to church, though Father didn't go in the morning because he had to do his rounds on the farm.

When we were wearing our Sundays we were under the strictest command to look after them. No tree-climbing, no bird's-nesting, no horsepond larks or ditch-jumping, and the Lord Himself wouldn't have had time to help us if we took out our catapults; Mother would have been in there with a couple of sharp lefts and rights. I can see, now, how good it all was. Good. We learned that if you didn't mean what you said and try to live up to it, then life could be a torment and a failure. My mother was not a person to tolerate either failure or disobedience.

Poor? No, I reckon we weren't poor. My four brothers and I found fun and enjoyment at every turn; it was known in the village that 'them young Moores' were of a larky disposition. Those were the days when, if you wanted walnuts or hazelnuts, you found a tree or bush and started climbing or bending it. For our autumn games, the conkers fell into our hands. There was always holly and mistletoe and laurel for Christmas, simply for the asking, and a million spring flowers, fresh and dewy bright, were there when we wanted them.

There were pets, too. We treated them kindly, though I reckon the only real way to be kind to a wild creature is to let it go. On the other hand, there seemed to be quite a few wild creatures that got on very well with man, like jackdaws, magpies, rabbits and mice; Spider (Henry) thought the same thing about that half-grown owl we once caught, but he changed his opinion right sharpish when it tried to make a meal of his right forefinger.

When Spider got that airgun, though (he'd swopped it for a set of glass marbles and a couple of grass snakes), we found that we were in business. First sight of anything we brought home was important. Mother was neutral about the gun, and Father said, 'First accident you have with that me lad 'll be your last.'

Spider had other ideas, and he'd no intention of telling Father. When no grown-ups were about he said to us, 'Can make some money.'

It had a sort of doubtful ring, that sentence. We were brought up to earn not much money for a fair old whack of work; 'making money' had a kind of illegal thrill to it. But we wanted to know how it could be done.

'Old Joliffe,' Spider said, 'we could make some money out of him.'

We couldn't believe it. Old Joliffe was the farm bailiff, a spectacled, whiskery man. Trunkie said it would be simpler to dig for gold at the bottom of our garden rather than go to Joliffe. But Spider led, and we followed. He took us into the farm, through the cobbled yards, and we walked to the great barn, where about a thousand sparrows were yelling pillip-chillip very loudly; whatever was happening, the sparrows didn't like it. When our eyes got used to the barn, a vast place with all sorts of farm machinery, we could see the cause of the noise. Old Joliffe had got the biggest ladder he could find, and was right up atop, near the beams, where he was using a long pole to poke out the nests from beneath the beams and ridges.

Spider spoke up. 'Hello, Mr Joliffe.'

Joliffe looked down from his perch, and his pole over-balanced him. He shouted and flung it from him just as his ladder stood straight-up vertically and started to fall away. He dived in an overturning sort of way, and landed with a flop and a curse in a big heap of hay and other small rubbish. We were so interested that we forgot to laugh, but when the bailiff surfaced and we saw his outraged face, we couldn't help it.

It didn't help Mr Joliffe any. He got out of the hay and shook his fist at the sparrows still screeching blue murder up above. He picked bits of straw off himself, and we gathered round and helped. Joliffe made mutterings under his breath. He was churchwarden, see, so he couldn't say it out loud, and I don't suppose we'd have learned anything if he had.

He said to Spider, 'All right then, boy. Every sparrow in here you get down, you'll get a penny. But I reckon that'd better be in your own time.'

We stared. Negotiations had been going on right underneath our noses. Spider slid a large wink at us.

'Gimme results, boy, that's all,' old Joliffe said, and lumbered off. We watched him go across to his office, converted from a stable at the end of the row.

I said, 'You're going to shoot sparrers up there, right at the top? It's so dark you could miss the roof. You'll not make any money like that.'

Spider gave me a shortish, pinched smile which implied that I was the junior in this quintet and why didn't I shut up? He said, 'Who can tell a barn sparrer from every other sparrer?'

After school the next day I went home and did a few jobs for Mam, then bolted out to find my brothers. I walked into the farmyard. If your father worked on the farm then bailiffs and gamekeepers expected to see his boys about, and they could go anywhere they liked as long as they obeyed the rules. I don't recall what the rules were, exactly, but they were all common sense; they had reason, and the great reason was that a farm had to live and thrive as a living unit, no waste, no extravagance, no unkindness. That's a good farm, any time in the present or past.

So, I found my brothers. They were doing a larking sort of jig dance, in which Spider, in the centre, had an air rifle in one hand and a sacking bag in the other. I went up and joined in. Then Spider stopped, and the others stopped and looked at me. 'What are you dancin' for?' Spider asked. 'You didn't do any sparrer shooting. You expecting some money, or something?'

'Why not?' I asked.

'Come to that,' put in Pudd'n (George), 'nobody touched that airgun 'cept Spider.'

We did some arithmetic, a bit spasmodic -- after all, this wasn't school stuff. It was a share-out of a successful commercial enterprize. We thought so, anyway.

'Fifteen sparrers.'

'Three each.'

'Threepence each, then.'

Spider scanned his brothers' faces, three determined and one hopeful, and gave in. 'All right. We'll not get fat on it at this rate, but it's a start, I reckon.' He looked hard at me. 'All right. Threepence each.'

'If we get it.'

'We'd better,' Spider said. He was afraid of nothing. We strolled across and dropped in to see old Joliffe. Spider displayed the lumps of bloodstained feathers which had once been sparrows. I turned away. I wasn't much for violence then just as I'm not now.

'Fifteen?' Old Joliffe fumbled in his pocket, found five silver threepences, and bestowed them like the king conferring a knighthood. We thanked him, and Spider put the sparrows back into the pieces of sacking.

'Hey, boy,' said the Bailiff. 'What you reckon you're gonna do with them sparrers?'

I never knew until that moment that we had a professional liar in the family. You should have seen Spider's face; it was like one of them cherubs on top of a church pillar. 'Sparrow pie,' he said.

Old Joliffe was vastly interested. 'Well,' he said, taking off his egg-shaped steel rimmed glasses and polishing them, 'I never heard tell of that lately. Not for years I haven't. Fancy that. All right, boy, take 'em to your mother with my compliments. Will yer do that?'

Spider said we would. When we got into the yard and out of earshot I started to speak, but Spider gave me a backhander which made my jaw vibrate right up to my earholes.

When we were in the lane, Spider took me by the lapels of my jacket. 'You tell Mam, and we'll make a pie outer you, Skimpy! You're getting a fifth of the money, so you mind your mouth!'

I minded my mouth. I minded it all through supper, pork fat spread on breadcrust, and I continued to think about it while my brothers slept, not troubled by anything, and dreaming, maybe, of all earning their livings as professional sparrow-catchers. I tried to reason with myself. Why kill sparrows? You kill a hundred, two hundred, you'll never notice the difference. And what good does that do to anybody? I could kill rats without mercy, stoats and weasels too, but sparrows? They were as common as people, and just as welcome.

Breakfast was a cautious meal. We had to be careful because we didn't know how our parents would feel about the sparrow hunting, and when it doubt we were careful. Mother, for instance, judged people by their 'attitudes': 'She's got a *nice* attitude' or 'I don't care for her attitude' and so on.

I couldn't ask my brothers at breakfast, and I stayed at school at dinner time with a few sandwiches. As soon as I could I clawed out, searching for news. I was just in time to see Spider knock one off the barn roof. I panted up. 'How many did you get today?'

Spider looked at me very hard, as though contradicting something I hadn't said. 'Twenty-five.'

I said; 'Your shootin's got better.'

'Hasn't it?' Spider said, and turned away.

We collected, and went and found Mr Joliffe in his dusty, fly-mucked little office. I watched Spider lay out the bodies,

twenty-five and an idea began to whisper at my mind. I thought
Spider was more on the make than he hinted.

Mr Joliffe polished his old glasses, put them on, and shoved
the greasy hat over his bald dome. He counted the sparrows. He
counted them twice, and then he looked up and stared a bit hard
at us. 'Twenty-five,' he said. He fumbled in his pocket.
'Fivepence each, then.'

We nodded. He found the pennies and handed them round.
'You enjoy that sparrow pie, then?'

'We did,' Spider said. The others of us nodded.

Old Joliffe picked up the sparrows one by one. I saw that some
looked fresh and plumpish, but most of 'em didn't.

The idea that I had germinated, took root, and flourished.

Joliffe's mouth was turned down, and he looked at us like the
local copper who once warned us off for trespassing. 'So,' he said,
very quiet and careful, 'as some of these are a bit stale-looking,
and you won't be wanting sparrer pie for a bit, I'll just take these
and get rid of 'em. Rats, you know. Mustn't leave carrion about
all over the place.' He waved a hand to dismiss us, and as we were
leaving he said; 'I shan't need any more sparrers. Reckon we've
scared a lot of 'em off, now. Word'll get around with 'em that
this farm ain't healthy.'

As I walked out with my brothers, I knew that Mr Joliffe had
spotted the trick.

We stopped in the lane. 'Eightpence each,' Spider glowered,
'eightpence each we got, for all that.'

'Could have earned a bob each in the time,' said George.
'Honestly, I mean,' he added.

We walked home together, a bit clouded over as you might
say. Spider said. 'If he tells Dad, we shall all get leathered. But,'
he added, 'anybody who breathes a word 'll get leathered by me,

too. If there's a name not to be mentioned in our house, it's "sparrer pie" Got that?'

We got it. We went in and nobody breathed a word and if Dad and Mam ever heard anything they never said. The funny tailpiece of this was that Joliffe went into sparrow hunting again, in his own way. He'd lay a 50 or 60 yard trail of corn, then wait around the corner. His gun held the smallest-shot cartridge he could get. He waited until he had fifty sparrows all in a row, and then he fired. But we never had sparrow pie, and I don't think anyone else did.

CHAPTER THREE

Joshua

I suppose that as boys we were more sternly treated than boys are today. Father only told us once; after that, he would use his belt to help our memories. We got very good at remembering. I don't see anything wrong with that: you have to keep a firm hand on a young horse until he knows the way, likewise with boys.

Now you take us five Moores and P.C. Boot, our local copper at the time. Our relationship with P.C. Boot was very harmonious, as long as he never heard us call him Old Booty – and we never did let him hear. If he ever caught us where we shouldn't be, he tanned us on the spot with an old gym slipper which he carried on his bike with his waterproofs.

We liked Old Booty's attitude, just as we fully understood the point of view of our parents. It was simple; you took a chance on doing something you shouldn't, and if you got caught then you either got father's belt, a couple of mother's backhanders or a drumming with Old Booty's slipper. The risks were calculated beforehand, and if it seemed worthwhile then we did what we wanted.

Yet we could be taken unawares, not by some little bending of the law, but because of the way we felt about animals. I remember, one beautiful May Sunday, getting near midday, we were moving cautiously through a wood. I didn't know this particular wood very well, though, as we single-filed through it, I felt that maybe my brothers did. It thinned, until we were on the edge of a clearing. They stopped, so I did too.

'Here?' asked George.

'That's it,' Arthur said.

'It's what?' I wanted to know.

'Sssssh!'

'That's the tree. Her with the big split up the trunk.'

'Shall I pick that caterpillar off your collar,' I asked him, 'or shall I let it wander?'

'Get it off!' Trunkie said. I got it off and waved it at him. He grabbed my nose with his first two knuckles, and twisted. Spider called us to order.

'See?'

'I see,' I said.

'The big twisted trunk. In the hollow.'

They'd been here before, and hadn't told me. Now they *were* telling me.

'Fox in there,' George said.

'See the hole, Skimpy?' Trunkie asked.

I began to have a feeling that . . . And it was Sunday, and we were wearing our 'Sundays'.

'Just your size, Skimpy.'

They knew they had me. They knew I'd love to have a fox

cub. They'd figured that they couldn't wriggle in there themselves, but little 'un could be brought there to have a go at it. My
Sundays. And on top of that I had a horrible nightmarish thought
of Skerrett, the gamekeeper, shoving his gun inside there and
letting go with both barrels, and me being shovelled out in
pieces.

'Got me Sundays on,' I said, and I knew, as I said it, that I
wouldn't get away with that excuse.

'Go on,' Spider said, 'I'll hold your coat for you.'

'And chuck in the towel too,' I said, sarcastically. It made no
difference. I took off my coat. 'All right.'

They were suddenly very brotherly.

'There, knew he would.'

'Brave for a little 'un.'

'We'll be proud of him.'

'Mam won't,' I said, 'not if I get my clothes mucky.'

'You won't.'

'In there and out like a breeze,' Spider said.

'Sweet as the breeze from Tomkins' corner,' I said. Tomkins'
Corner, you must know, was the wind guide in our village. You
could always tell which way the wind wasn't blowing, at least.
Tomkins had a pig for every square foot of ground, I reckon, and
he mucked them out about twice a year whether they needed it or
not.

'Listen,' I said, 'if I go, this cub's mine. We all share it, but I
own it.'

In the dappled wood we argued in hisses. There's no war worse
than a civil war, and no argument stronger than the ones you can
get between brothers.

Spider stopped the argument by seizing us in one armful and
banging our heads together. 'Look,' he said. 'Shut up, will you?

You'll have every fox and tomtit from here to Leicester running for its life. Let Skimpy do it, and we'll back him up.'

'Like pulling me out if I get jammed half-way?' I asked.

Spider ignored this. 'Go on, kid. The old vixen ain't in, for sure. Quietly, now.'

Spider had my measure; he knew I'd try, because I wanted a cub. And how could he tell that the vixen wasn't there? I don't know. Perhaps he was just bolstering up my courage.

I stalked over to the tree, taking what cover I could. It occurred to me that maybe no-one and nothing was in. But if the cubs were as small as my brothers said, then they'd be in there.

With only the very smallest difficulty, I slipped in through the opening. The smell of rotten wood mingled with the strong scent of fox. There wasn't much light. Suppose this was only the entrance to the earth, and it went down 20 or 30 feet?

Then suddenly I heard little whimpering noises. The cubs had smelt me. I put down a hand, then squatted. A cub nipped my finger, and in a moment I had him. He struggled and made little snarling noises.

I came out too fast for safety. First, I hit my head on a knobbly bit of wood, then when I got outside and started to bolt for the other side of the clearing, I slipped on a muddy patch. But I still had the cub, and trotted with him to where my brothers waited. They were all very cheerful, but I wasn't. I'd paid a high price for the little outing. I'd mud on my knees, and, twisting, I discovered a big streak of green on my backside.

I broke up the cub cuddlers. 'Oi!' I said. 'What about this lot?'

They thought nothing of it.

'Go on, kid, you can clean your knees.'

'That green ain't nothing.'

'Wear your coat over it.'

'That's it. Then Mam won't see it.'

'Won't she,' I growled. 'You know she can smell out anything like this.'

I spat on my handkerchief, and had a go at the mud on my knees. I got a result there, but with that streak of green I'd got trouble at the rear. But when I put my jacket on, it really did conceal the smudge. I thought I'd try and scrub it out with a soapy rag, or something.

'Can I take Joshua?' I asked my brothers. Funny, I'll swear that when I started the sentence I didn't know what I'd call him; the name just came.

Spider nodded. 'You got him, you take him.'

Holding back my eagerness, I took the little cub. He didn't struggle, now; he'd tired himself out. As I felt the quick thudding of his little heart, I could have signed the pledge against all forms of field sports, especially foxhunting.

We passed through the wood and climbed back over the fence into the road. Walking in a huddle with Joshua as the centre, we told each other that what we needed was 'A Plan'. The first thing was to settle the probable disposition of the enemy's forces.

'Dad'll be asleep inside.'

'Mam'll be at the back, with a chair inside the porch.'

'With the Sunday paper.'

'Means going a long way round.'

'Don't want 'em to be – what I mean is,' I said, 'that we don't want to catch 'em sudden, do we?'

'No,' said Pudd'n (George). 'And we don't want them to catch us sudden, neither.' Then he made a shocking suggestion. 'We couldn't go in *front* way, could we?'

We all gave him the frozen stare. Nobody went in through the front except very important visitors, or for weddings or funerals.

We were nearing our house. The nearer we got, the slower we went. We crouched along by the hedge, and peered over it. Trunkie said: 'Look. Go round by the front garden, hop across the path that'll be along Mam's line of sight, pass the lilac and whip him into the end hutch. How's that?'

I couldn't help thinking that the other inhabitants of Hutchville might not be too pleased with the new neighbour, as they were four rabbits, two magpies, a linnet and a guinea pig. Our new friend seemed quite content to be held and stroked. There was also the point that some in the village might not like us keeping a fox. We did know, though, that once we'd got him home and broken father into the idea of allowing him to stay, then anyone criticizing 'the Moore boys' would hear from Dad.

We arrived home in a series of short, agitated rushes, until we were almost up to our gate. The tension was terrific. Josh's heart was pounding too.

Then I was in with a quick scurry, round the front of the house, diagonally away from the side wall towards the hutches. And the first foot I put on the path was when mother called: 'Hey!'

Caught. Nabbed. With the goods on us. One word from Mam and we stopped dead in our tracks. We reluctantly gathered round in a semi-circle, with me and Josh as the centre of attraction.

My mother folded her arms. 'And what's that?'

'We found him.'

With sinking heart, I realized that we had chosen the wrong day altogether for fetching our new mate home. Dad slept in the big old windsor, Sunday afternoons, and if he was awakened, then somebody had better have a good reason for it. He was a firm sort of man, who used short words to say what he thought; they came out of him like shots from a rook rifle.

'Birds,' my mother said, 'alright, if they're not too big. Rabbits, fine. Even guinea pigs, as long as they're not left to smell. Linnets, all right again. Magpies, just about, as long as they ain't taught to swear. But foxes,' she said, 'foxes I won't have. Killers, foxes are. We'll have none of it,' she said. 'Take it away,' she said. 'At once,' she said.

We stood there trying to put on our pleading expressions. Then I overdid it, I started to cry. I cried loudly; I bawled.

'Will you be quiet!' snapped my mother.

I couldn't stop it.

'Frank! For heaven's sake, you'll wake your father.'

'Father's awake, alright, thanks to some as sees fit to break the calm of a good Sabbath,' my father said. He came through the kitchen to the porch with exactly the expression you'd expect to see on the face of a hardworking man who's been awakened.

He took one look. 'Take it back,' he said. 'Now,' he said, 'or I'll wring its neck.'

In a sad group, we drifted out on to the road again. Josh was quite peaceful, and licked my hand. The only thing on the credit side was that mother hadn't noticed how messed up I was.

Josh was a charmer; I'd known him barely more than an hour, and I knew that he'd have been my favourite of all favourite pets. I'd have looked after him so that he'd never have wanted to go back to the woods. I thought a bit and then remembered that Dad had said to take him back, but he hadn't said how *far* back. But after more thought I didn't see that that helped. It was an afternoon for being happy, the deeper hum of bees mingling with the dizzy sound of flies, and there were all the trees comparing their colours with a blue sky. And I nearly howled again.

But fortune was with us. We met Davy Fell. He said, 'Wotcha, Moores-O.' He saw the cub. 'Coo.'

It was already being said in the village that Davy had, variously, 'the hands' or 'the fingers' or 'a touch of the old man'. My father had 'hands' which knew how to touch and hold and be sympathetic. But in our bit of Leicestershire in those far-off days, to have 'fingers' meant that the animals you touched sometimes seemed to get well of their own accord. 'A touch of the old man', however, had a hint of witchcraft and warlockry.

As we told Davy the story, Josh wriggled to show that he wasn't necessarily in agreement with anything being said. We finished telling Davy, and Davy said, 'Let me take him.'

Joshua was transferred, and I can remember the pang I felt when I saw the cub become instantly peaceful.

'Joshua, his name is,' I said.

Davy smiled. 'Want me to take him?'

That was what we'd all been thinking.

'If I had him,' Davy said, 'you could come and see him any time.'

We all agreed that that would be a great idea, because we knew how good Davy was with animals, all wild creatures. We knew that he had recently mended a blackbird's broken wing, and the previous year he had fitted an accident-prone goose with a wooden leg, which worked fine until Christmas came along, and after that it didn't matter what the goose used for feet.

The end of the story pleased us all as far as Joshua was concerned. He behaved fine, walking on a lead just like a dog, seeming to accept us as acquaintances, but showing that he knew Davy was his master.

That year we had a sharp October, dry and much colder than usual. At Fell's farm the huge old kitchen was a favourite for some of Davy's pets, it was so warm. Because of that warmth, not only pets visited the kitchen; geese and ducks were occasional visitors.

One coldish morning Joshua was tied up to the copper boiler. With the kitchen door open on to the outside yard, two ducks popped in for a warm and a wander round. One popped out again sharpish.

Davy got there first. At the centre of the deadly flurry of fur and feathers were Joshua and the luckless duck. Davy could see that there was only one thing he could do. With one hand he cut Joshua free, and with the other he clouted the fox and made him let go of the duck, which lay bloody and kicking on the stone floor. All that really resulted was that the Fell family had duck a bit earlier than they'd bargained for.

'Mind you,' Davy said, telling us about it. 'I got the end of Dad's belt, but not as hard as you'd ha' got it, Skimpy, if it had been you from your Dad.' My father was noted for his stern discipline.

'When he goes to look for his family,' Spider said, 'he'll find they ain't there.'

'Hope he'll be all right,' Trunkie said.

'A young fox, fully grown?' Spratty said. 'He can look after himself, all right. No fox round here goes hungry.'

'That's right,' Davy said, rubbing his backside, 'and good luck to him.'

One little thing more; I tell it because it made me happy, and I don't care if I guessed right or not. It was a warm night in early November, and we had our bedroom windows open. I sat up with a start — it must have been about half-past two in the morning.

I could hear my brothers, giving the long low breaths of deep sleep. The church clock told me I was right about the time: only half-an-hour out. I could hear a dog whine, nearer to us than the church. I listened.

Quite close, no more than a hundred yards away, I heard the yap of a fox. I can remember a little tingle going down my spine as the sound was repeated; I felt my face smile. I knew who it was. Don't argue with me, because in this I brook no argument. Joshua had come to tell us that he was all right.

CHAPTER FOUR

From his Lair in the Morning

It was the winter coming before the following summer when we all upsticked to Lincolnshire. Therefore I am not strictly a Lincolnshire man, though nearly all my working life is associated with that county.

The countryman finds it very difficult to have a fixed view about fox-hunting. Only when we're able to interview the fox shall we get a worthwhile opinion. But my boyhood in Lincolnshire is tied up with fox-hunting.

I could plough at a very early age, under my father's strict eye. I can remember occasions when I've been driving the plough over those long, sweeping uplands, where you can see for miles; even today with all its crowding developments, there are still country views that take your breath away.

So. A still, sharp morning in November, when the sun's

struggling out, but can't yet cast the veils and give us a clear view. No sounds but country sounds. I can see myself behind a team of three jingling horses, and my father watching from the muddied stubble at the side. I'd raise my eyes from the turning earth and try to spot them at the first toot of a hunting horn. I'd stop the horses, shading my eyes, wondering what area they were going for. We'd look and listen, and maybe it was a long stretch of ten or fifteen minutes before we'd see them. Then we'd see them, in hunting pink and black, and I used to tell myself that not one of their magnificent horses knew how to plough. Sounds carried, and bounced back from the hills in faint echo.

Then, a change in the baying of the hounds. Now they had found a fox, and we'd try to guess which way he'd come. It was fine to see him, the way he twisted and turned, all cover his advantage, never letting them get downwind of him.

I thought then, and I think now, that the odds were stacked too high against the fox; I can remember once when, from my grandstand view, I saw a fox splash into a shallow woodland stream, and go along it for 50 or 60 yards; that one came off best, but mostly they didn't.

From sixty-odd years ago, I have in my mind clear and sharp a picture of the last few minutes of a fox. It is a picture of an animal who has run out, used all his energy. He ran across the big grass field where I was, a crouching, unsteady run, with his tongue hanging out and his brush hanging low. I saw him lie down, panting as though he would burst, as the sounds of the pack drew nearer (fifty-two to one, mark you, not counting humans). I saw that fox's eyes glaze over, as though some extra power was already preparing him for death, making it seem quicker and more bearable. Even so, his death was a horrible thing. I shall never change my mind from the viewpoint that a fox, too, has a right to live.

When we lived at Market Harborough I had to cross three grass fields, some of them with high hedges, to get back home from school. My dad was first horse man at a big farm nearby, a respected man because of his knowledge of horses. I can remember that we lived next door to the shepherd, a kind man who thought of his charges as creatures with likes and dislikes, needs and so on. If he ever thought of them as meat on the hoof he never showed it. On the other hand, he preferred mutton to other meats. One day as I approached I could see that there was a lot of hubbub and to and fro-ing in the road with horses, and the sound of many hounds. At last I got there, puffing and panting, and saw that there were two groups of people; one was the hunt and its followers, the other a crowd of locals, not liking what was going on by the sound of it.

I shoved my way to the front, and saw that the shepherd and my father were doing something to a big bit of drainpipe, which carried the water between two fields. There was a little bridge over it made out of three or four concrete slabs.

I found my sister Ada. 'What's up?' I asked.

'Fox is hiding somewhere down there.'

I looked round at the collection of noble lords and ladies, sitting on their fine horses and being called sir and madam, waiting for the local serfs to get the fox going again.

I heard my mother's voice call from somewhere behind, but I kept still and looking to the front because I wasn't going to miss this.

A voice of the high and mighty spoke from his richly-geared horse. 'Come along, Phipps. This is holding everything up, you know.'

Phipps, possibly the best huntsman in the county, returned the words with pithy interest. 'If you can do better, me lord, this is where the work is.'

A murmur of chuckles went through the crowd. They knew what Arthur Phipps thought of his lordship. Phipps had been offered nearly twice the wages he was getting from the local hunt.

My dad said: 'Here, we're doing this the wrong way. There's no need to dig. This ain't a complete section of pipe. Get the slabs up, and he's got to move.' I saw that as he spoke my father was eyeing the hawthorn hedge. It was thick, and about seven foot high.

Phipps pulled the bricks up with a squelching. Then they had to shift the slabs. I stood watching, and wondering at my father's glance.

Spectators commented.

'Idle bloody rich.'

'Go on, it's a sport.'

'Ask the fox, then!'

'Ought to be stopped.'

'Waste o' money, the whole thing.'

'If you don't like it, then don't stand here gawping.'

I ran forward to see, and as they knew that I was Arthur Moore's youngest they didn't stop me.

My father and Phipps heaved at the slab; it moved. The crowd gave an expectant mutter.

'And again,' my dad said. They shifted one, and then the other.

'Let it go your way, Phippy.'

Phipps stood holding the slab upright, its end resting on the ground.

I cannot, to this very day, shut out of my mind the memory of that fox's face. Anger and exhaustion, yes, but above all I saw a great fear, as the fated animal crouched along the muddy edge of the water. Yet, strangely, I hoped the fox was not dead yet.

I saw my father's hand sweep down to gather up the fox, and for a moment I thought that he was going to throw the animal over the hedge, and maybe give him a chance if he had the strength to take it.

Then someone shoved past me, just as my father was getting ready to throw the fox to his second chance. Donkin, the second huntsman called 'Hey, give him to me!'

My father was taken by surprise, and his hesitation gave Donkin all the time he needed. The second huntsman took the fox and, like a man putting a weight, he threw the creature into the crowd of dogs, and murder was committed on the Market Harborough Road. The dogs showed their true nature, the lords and ladies and hunting people showed their indifference, while the large number of people of no account (like us) used expressions of disgust and alarm. There was a lot there who'd never thought much before about the blood and guts side of fox-hunting. They thought about it that afternoon, no error. They had it thrust right under their noses.

Donkin was standing there looking sheepish, but generally pleased with himself.

My mother walked up and gave him a shove. 'I've a good mind,' she announced, in a voice as penetrating as any hunting horn, 'to give you a smack in the chops. Brute!'

Some said 'Hear hear!' and there was clapping and a bit of ragged cheering. Donkin backed away from her.

'He'll have had a few of your chickens, missis.'

'Don't care if he has,' said my mother, in that tone of voice which even my father treated with some respect. 'They're *my* chickens, and if I say he can have 'em, then he can. What cause did you have to get the poor beast killed like that? I'll still gi' you a smack in the chops!'

Donkin retreated a bit quicker, and mounted his horse. The M.F.H. was there and he never said a word, except to speak to his horse as he turned about. A way opened through the melting crowd. The horses and hounds walked over the blood-streaked road. A few people watched them go; a man called angrily to his sniffing dog. The shepherd stood with my father. He took his pipe out of his mouth, and spat his opinion of the hunt in their direction. 'Dang it, Arthur,' he said. 'I don't like to see that. Happen the varmint's had some of my lambs, I don't know. But I don't like to see that.'

I walked the few yards home with Mother, Father and my sister. At our door Dad paused, and looked into the clouding sky. 'It'll rain soon,' he said, 'and help clean up that mess down there.'

I asked, 'Dad, I could take a couple of buckets of water and —'

I stopped when I saw that my father was shaking his head. 'No boy, no.' He looked very solemn. 'Let Nature deal with it; she always does.'

CHAPTER FIVE

The Headstrong Filly

When we all moved to Lincolnshire just before the First World War my school career was over. I should have gone to the Lincolnshire school, but I didn't, and nobody bothered about it, and I started work. I worked with my father, and I was content.

The war touched us very little, at first. Later, it was to touch us greatly, and for my employer, and Ted Ramm, and me, it was an intolerable thing that came to plague us. The employer was Major Coulter, and the farm was always called 'Coulter's', and they'd been there for close on two hundred years. Ted was first horse man for the work horses, and I was second to him.

Coulter's didn't just farm; they bred bloodstock too, and this was the Major's chief concern, leaving the purely agricultural side to Waldron, the bailiff, who was easy enough to get along with. He knew his job thoroughly; the only thing that made me nervous was that he sometimes came to me to ask about the welfare of one particular horse, without prior reference to Ted.

He thought, you see, that young Skimpy (that's me) had the same 'hands' as his father.

This was a fine farm; there was money — most of it profit on the bloodstock side, I reckon — and they kept the place looking spotless. It was a farm with a fine old private house, too, screened by a double ring of close-growing beeches and cedars, planted long before the present house was built. So there I was, in a good job, still living with Mother and Dad, learning more and more each day, and Ted Ramm giving Father nothing but good reports of my work.

I should have been very happy; and so I was, until the arrival of Miss Elizabeth Clements, the Major's great-niece. She was about five foot four, with blonde hair tied back in a simple black bow; her eyes were brown. One look at her, and I felt as though a horse had kicked me in the head. No boy who's bothered about females not at all until he is past fifteen, ever got the pangs the way I did. I couldn't eat or sleep for thinking about her.

Spider had already gone to the war; the others were soon to go. We met at Dad's house for the evening meal, which, this particular evening, was a monster rabbit pie, enough and to spare. It was a family joke when Mother brought in the main dish for somebody to say: 'Well, that'll do for Frank. What's the rest of us having?'

I kept my eyes on my plate, and when my turn came I said: 'No thanks, Mam. I'm not hungry.'

The spoon fell from my mother's hand and clattered into the dish. There was a silence you could have hung your hat on.

'What?' said my mother, after ten seconds of hush. 'Don't want any? Did he say he didn't . . . want any?'

'Yes Mam,' I said, firm but polite, because my father wasn't yet past dealing out backhanders as far as I was concerned. The others — well, they looked at me as though I'd done something real anti-social, like trying out a pair of gelding shears on a cow.

My mother put a cool hand to my forehead. 'M'm,' she said, 'he does feel a bit heated.'

'No time for feeling sick,' said my father briskly, as though whatever it was could be cleared up at once if he gave the word. He addressed me. 'There's talk of Ted Ramm wanting to join up, even though he could keep out of the war legitimate.' He wagged a fork at me. 'That means you might get a rise.'

I reckon he expected me to cheer. I didn't.

'Horse man, at your age. That'd be something to live up to, eh? Me too, I'd have to live up to it as well. So you can't be sick. The farm can't spare you.'

As I got up and walked out, I heard mother say, 'Reckon he needs a good dose of castor oil.'

I listened for a moment outside the door.

'Give him brimstone and treacle as well, if you like,' Dad said, 'as long as he ain't ill.'

It didn't get better; worse, if anything. I got into the habit of lounging (me, lounging!) near the bloodstock stables, just on the offchance of her being around. She wore tan riding breeches and a white shirt, her hair always tied back and she looked as fresh as a breeze and as beautiful as spring rain.

Then one day she came and sought me out. I was cleaning a slapbox, and going really hard at it.

'Frank.' My heart missed a beat.

'Yes, miss?' The light from outside framed her in the doorway, and made her hair look like a halo.

'Can you come and look at Rajah?'

Elation at being asked was soon chased out of my mind by the sobering thought that this was something I'd better not do at any price. I'd have to put it to her very gently. There were work horses and bloodstock horses, and I was with the humbler but happier kind. Didn't she know? There was never anything actually said about this, but it was an unspoken rule that nobody questioned, nobody, that is, until she came.

I knew about Rajah. I'd seen him; black as coal and fiery as a furnace, he was. I asked, 'You got *him*, miss?'

'I'm riding him, along with others.' She nodded, a bit sharper. 'I have been riding since I was three, you know.'

I did a quick run round in my mind about any jobs left undone. 'Yes, miss. I'll come.'

We walked round to the bloodstock stables, homes of the aristocrats. 'What's the trouble, Miss Clements?'

'He has a wart,' she said. 'I think it's paining him. He's very restless. I wonder if you could do something?'

I thought quickly. 'Miss, you're going over the guvnor's head.'

'Am I?'

'Yes, miss. You'd be adding to his troubles. He's worried enough about the army requisitioners, just able to come and take what they want.'

She stopped and faced me steadily, her hands on her slim hips. 'You afraid, Frank?'

'Tain't a question of that, miss. It's a matter of what's right and what's wrong. I'm nothing to do with these horses; you should ha' known that, and not asked me. What's wrong with the vet? He'll come soon enough.'

'I've heard about you.' Now she snapped. 'Horse knowledge handed down, and you have 'hands'. I want your help. Are you going to refuse?'

I said, 'Make it an order, will you?'

She didn't hesitate. 'It's an order.'

Of all the horses we had, workers or fancies, Rajah was the one to keep clear of. I did hear that he once broke a groom's back with a kick, though that was before Major Coulter bought him. They'd had a dozen foals off him for themselves, and as many again for other breeders.

I walked behind Miss Clements to Rajah's stable. She called him, and he looked out; she cooed at him, stroked him, and that wild-eyed brute was clay in her hands. To show me how gentle he was, she let him take a lump of sugar from her lips.

'Look,' she said, 'his lower eyelid. You see?'

I saw alright. Rajah had one of the biggest warts I've ever seen on an animal. It was red and angry, and the eyeball was inflamed, and here she was, calmly passing on to a lovesick boy a job which would have made the vet hum and ha a bit.

'Well?'

'Biggest one I ever saw, miss.' I was being slow and deliberate, imitating father when he needed thinking time.

'What are you going to do about it?'

'Warts are tricky things, miss.'

'Then you be tricky, and let's have a cure.'

'I reckon I can put him right, miss, but you'll need to have him held down. Roped, to be safe.'

'Nonsense.' She sounded arrogant. 'Rajah obeys me. Get your cure, I'll see he behaves.'

When I got home, I asked my father.

'Wart?' he said. 'Well, that needn't be difficult. I'll look in my cupboard.'

I didn't go with him to his cupboard. Nobody did. He came back with a small pot. It was half full of a grey ointment. He had the lid between thumb and forefinger when he stopped and looked hard at me. 'That Rajah. He's never a work horse?'

'No.'

'Then what're you doing, doctoring him? He's not in your charge. Where's your manners, boy?'

I explained to him carefully, stressing some things and playing down others.

'H'm,' Dad said. 'Now, first thing is, none of this must get in his eye. Let that happen, and you'll have real trouble on your hands. So don't you let me down, boy.' And he completed his instructions.

Next day I was on pins and needles waiting for a sight of her, fearing that this whole thing might be blamed on me. I was sitting on a bucket outside the chaff house eating a sandwich, when suddenly there she was.

'No, Frank, don't get up. You finish your sandwich.'

I finished it. I took out the little jar and showed it to her. I'd already selected the other item needed. She was looking at me seriously. 'Frank, I rode by Postland station this morning. Early.'

'Did you see Sam, miss?' Sam Congreve was the signalman at the little station. He was, you might say, chief of the local wire service. He got facts when he could and rumours when facts were scarce.

'I saw Sam. The requisitioners will be here on Thursday or Friday.'

'Oh my Lord,' I said, and I wasn't being irreverent. It really was like a prayer. 'It's a quiet walk by night then, is it, and temporary stabling at the places where the military have already been?'

'Perhaps it's not as simple as that. Sam Congreve said that he'd heard a rumour that all the byways would be covered, and all the night walkers would be trapped. Then it can mean fines, imprisonment even.'

'Miss Clements, it ain't possible for 'em to know all the byways. You got to be bred to it, live here for years. Why, I swear that I don't know half of 'em yet myself.'

I thought of my own charges first. If the military took many we'd be sunk. But we'd have to let them have *some*. You just had to be careful how you let 'em pick and choose, after you'd sent a reliable half-dozen men down the lanes, byroads and paths, to where they could stable them in safety at some place already visited by the robbers.

She led me to the bloodstock stables.

I said, a bit nervous, 'Where's everybody, miss?'

She knew what I meant. I was scared of having someone find out. I oughtn't to have been, because she would have stood by her order. 'Uncle's at the station, and Waldron's off to Holbeach. Show me what you're going to do for Rajah.'

I told her, showing her the little pot of ointment, and the horsehair for tying the wart. I warned, 'None of this ointment must get into his eye.' Then I added, 'That was right what I said, miss. He ought to be roped. Why didn't they send for the vet?'

'They did,' she said, and I was shocked, suddenly all on my own. 'He put some oily stuff in and around the eye. Did no good. Come on.' She walked off with her head high, her hair like a crown in the sun, and her riding crop slap-slapping against her boots.

When we got there, Rajah was looking out. One sight of that eye gave me the trembles. The wart was not actually within the lower eyelid, but it looked nasty, and I wasn't fond of Rajah's mean expression either. But it meant nothing to her. She patted and stroked him, gave him a sugar lump, and he was quiet as a lamb. This was a job to sort out the men from the boys, and I was still very much a boy.

'Well?' she spoke quietly, and put a lot into the one word. 'Are you afraid, Frank?'

'Yes, miss.'

'Of Rajah? Look at the beauty.'

'I'm looking. And I did say he ought to be roped.'

She turned, gave me a long look, and then stroked Rajah again, making cooing noises at him. Still looking at the horse, she said, 'Come on, Frank. This is where you grow up.'

I went forward. It was as though she had hypnotized him. That horse stayed almost like a statue. I took the tiniest scrap of that ointment, and applied it to the wart. Then I took my horsehair, and looped it ready. She didn't look at me, she watched Rajah. I'd got the ready looped horsehair in my lips. My prayer was a curse, but said to myself. 'Now, you beautiful bastard, hold still.'

I pulled the loop down to a bit less than half-an-inch across, put it down over the wart as far as it would go, and then tightened until I got real resistance. I tied, tied again, clipped the end.

'Must go, miss,' I said, abruptly, 'I'm not supposed to be here. And there's work to be done.'

She called, 'Thank you, Frank.'

I hurried off.

As I made for the stable yard (my stable yard, I mean, not the one where the fancies lived) I heard the Major's Daimler. I stood to watch him pass, but he pulled up beside me. He was a pink-faced man, with white hair and moustache, and eyes that were blue and steadfast. 'Where have you been, Frank?'

'Miss Clements asked me to help her for a bit, sir.' I saw him frown. 'There'll be no neglect in the work horse stables, sir, you can be sure o' that.'

'I know. I've watched you, boy. There's bad news, Frank.'

'The robbers, sir?'

'The military requisitioners, Frank. The officer and his men will be along very soon, now. Perhaps even today. You ready?'

'Yes, sir.' I knew the walks by night for hiding horses from the military. 'But you'll have to let 'em take some, sir.'

He was a cheerful man, a bit peppery, but generally cheerful. He wasn't like that now. 'One thing that makes me so angry . . .' He let the thought trail away. 'Yes. We shall have to let them have some. Frank, there's not a working horse we can spare.'

I can see him so clearly, even now, leaning on the side of the Daimler, while all around blossoms crowded blossoms. 'No working horses to spare,' he repeated.

I got his drift then, and didn't believe it. But with his next sentence I had to believe it.

'I'm going to offer all the bloodstock, try to do a deal with the vet officer. I feel that if — if I'm straight with him, he'll understand.'

It sounded scary to me, but I liked the idea of all the work horses staying. 'Taking a chance, sir.'

'I've taken chances before, boy. I was at Mafeking.'

'All the blood horses, sir?'

He nodded. It had cost him a lot to make that decision. It showed. 'And if I seem bad-tempered these days, Frank, give me a bit of latitude, boy.'

'Yes, sir.' This was the longest he'd ever spoken to me; I felt I was leaving the boy's world for the man's. I didn't speak of Miss Clements' temper and what she might say at Rajah's being included in the army lot.

A voice called from the farm track which led down from the road. He was a tall uniformed figure with a long stride. 'Hello, Major Coulter.'

The Major turned and shaded his eyes. 'Who's this?'

The Captain was a handsome young fellow in his middle twenties.

'Drat my eyes,' the Major said, 'it's young Stevens. Captain, RAVC. So you did pass those exams after all.'

'I did, sir. And for that I'm ordered to select horses for God knows what kind of work. Is Beth here, sir?'

'She is. She makes play of the work, fortunately for me. Your parents moved, didn't they?'

'Yes. To Boston.'

I muttered an excuse and walked away. I thought that there might well be trouble when that young officer found what a stubborn one Miss Clements was. Still, as they were both about the same class of people I supposed they'd understand each other. I hoped that Miss Clements might be able to keep him away from checking on the work horses that same day, so as to give us a chance to walk a few by night.

That night, we walked three to old Tullet's farm. He was a good old chap and, like the rest of us, he took the view that you can't run a farm without horses. It wasn't only that; in the RAVC there were some who thought that the way to train horses was to break their spirits, and who used to love the lash to show the horses who was boss.

In all that countryside there was no man working on a farm who was not filled with gloom about the horses being taken. The yard of Postland station filled, emptied, filled, emptied, and men watched their horses go and cursed, or wept, or did both, and not for the simple reason only that it was money out of their pockets. Real farm men know that the land is a heritage, not just a source of money, and not too much of that, either.

Still, at our place, Captain Tony Stevens wasn't in a hurry. Ted Ramm said to me, 'He's friendly is that young vet captain.'

'Trust him?'

'Far as I could throw a sack of taters, yes,' Ted said. He was mid-twenties, black-haired, chest and arms, thickish, tough. A sculptor might have thought him a good subject. 'What I mean is, Frank my boy, that he's a bit too handy with the charm. Like a show horse what gets the idea it's always on show.'

'M'm?' I was doing some brasses and listening to the violence of a thunderstorm outside. My mind kept going back to Miss Elizabeth Clements.

'Ramm.' It was the Major coming in, shaking the wet off his tweed hat. 'No, don't get up, boy. You carry on.'

I dared a question. 'Is it about the horses, sir?'

The Major avoided our direct gazes. It was something he wasn't very happy about. He said, 'They can pick the hunters and so on as they want. Ah – they think that we have only eleven work horses, by the way. I want you to understand, Ramm – and you boy, as you're here – that I don't like this; but I find my justification in the evasion because the whole system of horse priorities is wrong.'

He was frowning at the floor. I dared a question. 'Rajah too, sir?'

'I know Miss Clements is very fond of him but I'm not making any exceptions.'

'Could you be dead certain, sir' Ted asked, 'that a fine mount like Rajah would ever get to France?'

The Major's face seemed to sag, and he looked older quite suddenly. 'I know what you mean. This is no sort of a deal. Gold for dust and life for death. Don't you ever dare think that I like it.'

'Letting Rajah go, sir. Ain't it like making bread of next year's seed corn?'

'My decision, Ramm. I wish some of those organizers could understand what a sacrifice we're making.'

Ted said, quite simply: 'I was at Postland this morning, sir, watched 'em loading. Met Jack Collins, from Seabank farm.' Ted's face was set, his mood matching the Major's. 'Jack was weeping, sir.'

The Major nodded, stayed with his dark thoughts for a moment, then straightened up, gave us a brisk good morning, and left.

Later that morning Ted and I went across to the farm kitchen, where there was usually some tea available. This was quite all right with the Major; he was not a man for pinpricks and niggling detail. If you did your job, then little liberties were allowed. As we crossed the yard in the glorious sunshine which the shower had left behind all I could think of (next to Miss Clements) were the horses soon to be taken from us.

The doorway of the farm kitchen was twined about with pale mauve wisteria; it was beautiful. We took our tea and sat on the old cornerstone looking down the farm track. 'Hey,' Ted said, and nodded to where two people riding horses were approaching. Miss Clements was on Rajah, Captain Stevens rode Starlight, an older, quieter horse, but very handsome. 'Look well, together, don't they Frank?'

My heart was breaking. 'Yes,' I said.

They had some conversation with each other when they stopped about 50 yards away, and then the Captain turned about, and Miss Clements came up to us.

Miss Clements called me to her. 'Frank, will you help me?'

'Yes miss.'

'But you don't know what it's about.'

'Won't be nothing bad, miss. So I'll help.'

'It's about Rajah.'

That was no surprise at all. 'Yes, miss.'

'We are going to save him from the horse thieves.'

Damn me, I thought, she's pretty friendly with one of 'em. Or is that part of the plot – finding out what they're going to do? Or maybe that Captain Stevens is in it along with her . . . ?

'It'll be risky, Frank.'

'It won't, miss.' I indicated Rajah. 'No risk, as long as I keep in front of this feller.'

'There's a horse train taking all our bloodstock leaving Postland station at three tomorrow morning.'

Stevens *must* be in this with her, I thought. But I wouldn't dare ask. 'That's the train Rajah won't be on, is it miss?'

She dismounted, came to me to talk quieter. 'What's the difference between Starlight and Rajah?'

'Lots.'

'Not at three in the morning with his white blaze blacked out.'

I gaped a bit. 'They can count, miss, can't they?'

'Not if they think we've nineteen bloodstock horses, instead of twenty. Could you black out Starlight's blaze?'

'What about hiding Rajah, until they've gone?' I thought of a place as soon as I'd said that. Through the field entrance to the stables, and across to – 'the old shearing barn.'

She smiled. We understood each other. I did wonder, seeing that this operation was Captain Stevens' responsibility, how she was going to get away with it. Still, I suppose he could leave it to his men, in charge of the warrrant officer, once the plan was made and the cargo manifests were ready.

She said, 'The other grooms and the soldiers will walk them down to Postland, and I shall take Captain Stevens down to the station in the Daimler.'

'It's chancy, miss,' I said.

'So is crossing the road,' she answered. 'You've taken risks before, Frank. Now take another one. We'll all take another one, for Rajah.'

That was the plan, then. Maybe she was taking it calmly, but I wasn't. I was like a flea on a firebar the whole day. I jumped when spoken to, scrambled through my work, forgot to do all sorts of routine things, until Ted Ramm fairly lost his temper.

'I dunno, really I don't,' he growled. 'I thought you was going to be a good and sensible lad, Frank, and look at you, no more sense of responsibility than a mare in season! Much more of this and I'll have to have a word with your father. You ain't yet too big for a good leatherin'!'

At dusk I was ready. I took some dye, and some rag for dabbing it on. Feeling like a criminal, I chose the long way round so as to get into the bloodstock stables from the field entrance. There I stopped, and looked. It was too quiet. Before I could sort out the emotions that were roaring through my mind, a figure loomed up out of the creeping twilight.

'Oi.'

'Hello, Ginger,' I said. He was older than I was, going on seventeen.

'You don't work here.'

'No. Got a little job to do.'

'Who for?'

I told him. 'Oh, her. Ah. Her and that Captain Stevens. Not fond of him. Too cocky and snappy with his own men *and* the

Major's. I wouldn't buy a horse from him, not without a second opinion. She's real gone on him, I reckon.'

There was silence. 'Ginger, where's the horses?' I was nervous, now. Ginger had made a thought I'd had for some time grow into a worry.

'Why, they've gone. Taken.'

It was like being hit between the eyes. 'Gone?'

'Ah. All be down at Postland station now.'

A bat fluttered over us and changed course half-a-dozen times in as many seconds. I watched it stupidly.

'Him and her's having a twilight ramble,' Ginger said. 'Well, I got to go. If I've no job here now I reckon I'll join the army. So long.'

He walked away, and at the white gate the coming dark swallowed him. So there I stood, a daft and stricken lad in the middle of the gloom of that spotless stable yard. I was thinking hard, though. Miss Clements was no fool, not about horses anyway. What she felt about Stevens might be another matter altogether, but Rajah would come first. If she heard that the horses' leaving was put forward, she'd somehow get Rajah to the old shearing barn, remembering what we'd said. She must have done this. Then, growing bigger in my mind, was the question of this vet captain. Was he being straight with her?

Voices came, soft in the growing dark, and then idling footsteps. I squatted in a corner of the yard. The ground was now dark, but up above the sky still swam in light. I recognized the voices. Elizabeth, and the Captain, as Ginger had said. I couldn't help hearing; anyway, I listened without shame.

'Darling,' he was saying, 'don't take it too much to heart. I'll be back. And you saved Rajah, didn't you?'

So, she'd told him where Rajah was. That shouldn't have mattered, but somehow it did, to me.

She said, very softly, 'You don't have to go just yet, do you?'
'Not yet.'

I could just hear; my own feelings I can't describe. I heard a
latch noise. 'Let's stay here a while,' she said. Straw rustled; the
end stable was kept as a store. I heard the latch go again.

By now I was feeling a bit shaky, but in my mind, like a dark
tunnel, there was a speck of light at the end. I had to follow that
speck of light, no matter what Miss Clements thought of her
Captain Tony Stevens. For me, the thing was to make sure that
she got treated right. I didn't know to what time the departure
had been advanced, but I did feel that I hadn't got a couple of
hours to spare.

I made my way into the first paddock. One or two lights on
my right, from the village, one or two in the main farm
buildings to my right rear. I hurried along by the thick old
hawthorn hedge which would soon need trimming and layering,
and found the stile. I climbed over it, and went on, fast but
steady, trusting to my memory of obstacles now invisible. I
slowed as I approached. A piece of old slate rattled under my feet,
and I thought I heard an answering noise, more clattery, as
though made by the hooves of a horse.

'Rajah. Rajah old boy.' You had to have a firm voice for this
one. I made my voice so firm that I believed in it myself.

I went closer to the door, peered in, saying his name softly.
Gradually, I became accustomed to the dark of the barn, which
was near total. I walked in, still saying his name, found his head
and patted him. I nearly laughed at the thought I had – 'Thank
God he's not in the biting mood, tonight.' I gave him a couple of
pieces of sugar, and untied his halter. Then, hoping that time
was on my side, I led him out and away, through the copse and
up the little bit of rising ground which was probably an island in

the marsh a thousand years ago. I tied him up with his halter again and gave him my last piece of sugar. Then, feeling as though I'd got a glow in the middle of my gut, I hurried off. I could have been home in fifteen minutes if I'd wanted, but I didn't want. I was going to see this thing through, and show up Captain Stevens for what he was!

I got back to the old barn just as the village clock struck eleven. I sat down, hidden by a big clump of herb robert. And I waited. Just after half-past eleven I heard the voices of the expected visitors, grumbling, also as expected.

'Join the bloody army,' growled a voice, 'your King and Country need you.'

'Ah, and come looking for a horse while the Captain has a bit of that there.'

'How'd yer know?'

'Stands to reason. Last night here and goodbye Dolly, I must leave you.'

'He'll give us a medal for this, finding his poor straying gee-gee.'

'You won't get a medal if we don't find it.' They paused. One lit a cigarette.

'This is the barn then, ain't it?'

'Looks like it. Watch out for them stinging nettles.'

I heard the rattle of feet at the entrance. I stayed for just a moment. A quartering owl drifted silently above me and something scurried by in the clump of wildflowers. Then I left; I'd heard enough.

My night was not yet done, though. I still had a duty to complete. Stevens wanted Rajah for his own, but he was careful and cunning. I should have warned her that the old shearing barn was too easy a place to get at, and too near for a safe hideaway until the soldiers had gone. But then that would have shown her what I really thought of her Captain, and she would have taken me for a vengeful boy, not for someone who aimed to be a man.

So I went back and found Rajah, and we both waited until the whistle from Postland told us that a new consignment of four-legged cannon fodder was on its way to the front. Then I led Rajah back to his own stable, the only horse in the bloodstock yard now, and saw that he was comfortable. There were no lights. All was quiet.

Even then I couldn't go home. I had to look inside that store, where she had been with him. Daft, of course, but I couldn't resist it. A faint gleam of something white caught my attention. I picked it up. It was a small scented handkerchief. Then I went home.

I had a chance to go to the bloodstock stables the next morning. She was in the yard fondling Rajah. She saw me and she smiled, a bit sadly.

'Good morning, Frank.'

'Good mornig, miss.'

'You brought him back, eh? That was clever of you, realizing I'd hide him myself when the train departure time was put forward.'

'Didn't take much working out, miss.'

'Well, thanks anyway, for saving my beautiful.'

What could I say to her, knowing the grief that the truth could cause her? She never suspected his double-dealing, while he at once saw through hers. I kept my mouth shut.

CHAPTER SIX

Jenny

One morning in early October my employer arrived at the stables, his hand held by the prettiest little girl you ever saw. She was about seven, she had her dark hair cut in a straight bob, blue eyes and a button nose. She made the sunshine brighter.

'Jenny, this is Mr Moore, who looks after all the horses.'

She smiled and shook hands very politely. 'Good morning Mr Moore, I'm pleased to meet you.'

'Good morning to you Miss Jenny. And what do you think of our farm?'

'I like it very much, thank you. This is my safety tour,' she added.

My employer said, 'Just showing her where she may and may not go. Can't have her climbing the fence and trying to feed grass to Banger, can we?'

Banger was the bull, and the list of people entitled to approach him was short.

'That we can't,' I said.

Jenny was one of those kids who are never still. She was jigging and hopping and wandering round and peering at and into things.

'Will your father be able to come along and do that little job?' my employer asked.

'He'll come,' I said. 'I'll remind him. His usual, five bob a time?'

The firebell rang; it had been rigged up so that anyone in the house could call him to the telephone.

'Frank, you look after Jenny, will you, while I answer that?' He went off briskly.

As I was now left with Jenny, and didn't have anything vital to do for fifteen minutes, I carried on where my employer had left off. 'Shall we go roads way or fields way?'

'Fields, please.' She didn't walk much this little one. She kept running ahead and dancing and pirouetting, coming and taking my hand for a little while, then dancing off again.

'What safety precautions have you learned so far, Jenny?' She chased some wind-scurried leaves for a moment.

'I must shut gates all the time. The barn can be dangerous with all the implements there. I mustn't fall into the pig sty, fluster the chickens or be rude to the bull.'

By now we had left the farm buildings behind us, and we opened and carefully closed a gate behind us.

'Calves,' I said, pointing to a group of young Friesians. 'Hey, come here,' I called, 'don't you run at them like that. Go steady.'

'Is it because we haven't been introduced?'

I couldn't help chuckling at that. What a life it must be, to be seven years old on a bright October morning. 'That's right. Now, if you walk slowly up to them and hold out a handful of grass, they'll come to you, like this.'

I showed her. She was delighted, commenting that they were wide eyed and breathy-snorting (I liked the last one) and saying that she'd like one for herself. She sorted out the one that was getting most patting and seemed to like it most, a little bull calf. 'There, see? He likes me!' More grass was hurriedly picked. 'Mr Moore, has he a name?'

'You find him one.'

She was thrilled. She asked the calf, 'What would you like?'

'Why not call him Cracker?'

By her expression I could see I'd gone up in her estimation. 'Why Cracker?'

'Because the bull's name's Banger.'

She giggled and danced. 'Ooh, yes, that would be lovely.' She gave the calf a wide smile. 'Cracker, that's you, that's what your name is, and I'll come and see you every day, won't we, Mr Moore?'

We made our way back to the farm. I said, 'You be guided by your Uncle William, eh? Do as he says.'

We were at the gate when we turned and saw that Cracker had followed us. It took us a full five minutes to say goodbye to him.

'Pretty as our two girls,' I told the wife when I got home.

'Who's she belong to?'

'Stevens, Holbeach way.' I thought a bit about that and I went digging into a memory that must have placed the name in my mind fifteen or sixteen years ago. 'Stevens the vet's daughter. Seem to remember him from during the war.' That was a memory that wasn't easily got rid of, it if *was* that certain Stevens. 'Could be the Stevens who was going to marry old Clements' great niece, and didn't. Wartime, when the Major gave up all his bloodstock.'

'Ah, that war. Glad you missed most of it.'

I found a woodbine which had got into a waistcoat pocket. I lit it. 'Ten minutes with this and the paper, and I'll be off back.'

I had never before seen such an attachment between animal and human being as grew between Jenny and Cracker. A little grass, some kind words, and everywhere that Jenny went the calf was sure to go.

Watching her, my employer asked, 'Think it could be dangerous, Frank? She's really very fond of him. Might he turn on her?'

'An animal might do anything. But as for it being safe, I wouldn't like to say. It wouldn't worry me a lot if she were mine.'

When we had this conversation, he was in his car, about to go to Boston. 'She's a bit wilful and spoilt, pretty as she is.'

He turned his attention to another car, an ancient Model T, which approached with a chuff and a clatter. A tallish young fellow got out, picked up a load of photographic gear, and came towards us. 'Ah, you'll be the owner, sir?'

'Where are you from?'

'Eastern Counties Papers. May I take a picture of the little girl who leads the calf about everywhere?'

Employer and I exchanged glances.

'Sure fire stuff you know, sir. Children and animals, you can't go wrong. Do I have your permission?'

'Frank, you be there just in case there's any problems. Can you manage it? I must get off, now.'

He left, leaving me with the photographer.

'Put all your gear back into the car,' I said, 'and drive me out to the field road, and we'll find the little maid.'

'With the calf?'
'Mostly where she is, he is.'

After the pictures were published, in two national papers as well as the regional dailies, I began to feel (rather than think) that something was either going wrong or had gone wrong. I didn't know, for example, that the newspaper people had got permission from my employer to have the calf taken into the village and take some pictures of her there, including one of her offering Cracker a lick of ice-cream. All very well if the owner wanted that, then nobody argued.

But I thought a little; I hadn't ever before experienced what 'turning somebody's head' really meant, until I saw false pride and petty arrogance increasing daily in Jenny's manner. She still looked the charming nipper I first knew, but she was daft for that bull calf; I reckon the one knew as much about life as the other, and ignorance was bliss.

'Three o'clock this afternoon, Frank, if that's convenient to your father,' said my employer. 'I'll fetch him if you like.'

'No,' I shook my head. Crippled as Dad now was with arthritis, he'd sooner walk to prove that he still could get about, even though the effort grew daily.

'Want any men?'

'No, not for calves. Just Dad and me. Get him in a corner with his head over the manger, he won't shift. We always manage bull calves easily.'

'You could do the job as well as he can.'

'Maybe,' I said, 'but when illusions are all you have, you'll die if you lose 'em.' I added, 'I do know a fair bit about horses, and learned nine-tenths of it from him. But when he's about, there's a touch of electricity in the air. All the animals know he knows about 'em.' I remembered, then. 'What about young Jenny? We'd better not start while she's around, had we?'

'I thought about that. Her parents are picking her up about two, and your father'll be along about three. So that's all right. I'll see she says goodbye to Cracker before lunch.'

I had learned much from my father, and some thought that I was just as competent. I knew I wasn't. In some things I might equal him, but in spite of his advancing years he was still the boss. When we did bull calves, he would never use shears, he preferred his old knife, razor sharp, from which wounds he said recovery came quickest. He preferred me to be there while he did the cutting. Even with horses he still used a knife, and though he showed me the correct way with other male animals the horse's gelding he never showed me.

As I walked to meet my father, I could see that this was one of his good days, when he could afford to make his little jokes about 'old Arthur's old arthuritis', or 'should have had my name changed. Name I've got's an open invitation to the blasted affliction.'

''Lo, boy.'

We walked along to the farm, where my employer greeted him respectfully; though I reckon he took no account of the stories that my father had 'a bit of the Old Man' in him (the 'Old Man' being the devil), he did recognize my father's well-deserved reputation. The only times I ever remember when Father's opinion was compared with the vet's, father was right.

My employer said, 'Her parents should be here soon Frank.' He gave me a significant look and nodded at Jenny. Soon they arrived, there was lots of family chit-chat, and then the last goodbyes were said. She said for me to give her love to Cracker. I said I would. Nobody told her that, in half-an-hour, Cracker would be a sterile bullock and, not much later, beef.

Half-an-hour later, after a lot of grunting and sweating, we'd done two bullocks, and very neatly. My father gave his order (yes, order is what I mean) that these two should be apart from each other and from the rest of the cattle to be certain the wounds healed properly.

Bill Turvey, a large muscular man who was an amateur weight- lifter brought Cracker along and called us; we went outside to see, and certainly Cracker was a lot friskier than the other two had been.

'This 'n, Frank?'

'Ah.'

'Strong 'un.'

'We can handle him.'

'No point in sweatin' when we needn't. This one's got more spirit than's good for him.' He felt in his pocket. 'Takes a bit of seed cake, does he?'

'Used to from the little maid.'

My father unwrapped a piece of rag in which were lumps of seed cake. He gave one to Cracker, and followed that almost immediately with the doped one. He said to Sam, 'Walk 'un about a bit, boy. Five minutes should be about right.'

Five minutes it was. All Cracker's punch and go was out of him, then.

'Is he going to flop out?' I asked.

My father glared. 'I give him just enough; think I don't know?' He picked the right knife. 'Now, get his head well into that corner, and over the manger.' The knife had a bow curve in it; it was very old and very good steel.

I got Cracker wedged so that he couldn't move.

'Ain't never mangled one yet, but I suppose there's always a first time,' my father said. 'Now, keep him still. Ready?'

The calf gave a great intake of breath when he felt the knife, and he seemed to give another before letting out with – well, it was more of a howl than a bull noise, a great shuddering cry. I'd heard 'em roar before, but never before had I heard the rending cry which came from this one.

'Leave go,' my father said, 'and let'n stand natural. Watch him, though.'

Sam Turvey, who was standing by in case extra strength was needed, said, 'I'm glad little Jenny went before we started this. If that child –'

There was another cry, a strangled, windy kind of noise. Jenny, rigid with horror, was standing in the doorway. (I learned later that she'd left her big Teddy Bear behind, and insisted on her parents coming back to fetch it). Poor, poor child. She had her mouth open and was forcing out air too hard, at the start, to get out the waiting scream. But when she did it was a most dreadful noise. I picked her up, kicking and squealing as though she was being killed; she was so hysterical that I wondered if I should duck her in the horse trough.

Fortunately, her parents heard and came running. The vet, lately Captain Tony Stevens RAVC, got there first. 'For God's sake, what did you do to her?' Her mother came and led the child away, still screaming and sobbing. I told her father.

'My God,' he said, 'she could have bad dreams for years.'

My employer came up; farm work had come to a temporary stop as various heads peered in our direction. 'We can't blame anyone for this,' he said, 'we thought she was out of the place for good.' Stevens turned on his heel and left, hurrying after his wife.

My father came along, snapping his case shut. He was pleased. He liked to show that he was still master of one of his many skills. He was sorry about Jenny. 'Poor little maid, to come and see that.' He shook his head. 'No animal's worth her sort of fear.'

I asked, 'Not horses, Dad?'

My father gave me one of his steady looks. 'You ain't a fool, boy. You know horses are special.'

CHAPTER SEVEN

Break it Gently

Breaking in a horse is a skilled mystery. You either break him (in the bad sense) or you make him. We start on him when he's a two-year-old; plenty soon enough, you don't want to overdo things. You must get that animal so that it can deal with anything you put him to, long gear, traces, shaft work, and so on, and then turn him out until he's three years old. Even when you've trained him don't overload him with work before he feels ready to work full-time. Use him for a day here and there. When you're training, you mustn't throw your weight about and shout. If you do, then he'll see in your bad behaviour all men for all times, and he'll become worth nothing except for dog meat, and you don't want that.

First, you have to get him a mouth; that is, you put a bridle on, and a special bit with keys in it for him to bite on. Let him get the gradual feel of this for about a fortnight, on and off, so as to accustom him to it. Once you've given him a mouth, even if it is a bit tender, then bring him out to the grass field on a good long rope. Put a collar on him, but don't give him a blinkered bridle, just a slip, so that he can see all round him. Collar on, traces on, and be careful how you put the traces on. He's still nervous, so don't just sling on the traces sharply, but be gentle, talk to him. He's got to develop that trust in man.

Take him out in the grass field, and link him to a heavy piece of wood, like an old railway sleeper. Chain him to that, and then put on the sleeper a wooden heeltree, about a yard long with an S hook in the middle. Hook that on to the chains, and then lead him round and round, and make him stop against that heeltree. You can't back him, remember.

When he's on, you have a ten-yard-long rope. When he feels those traces, he'll want to gallop away, and he'll go round and round on the rope. Let him gallop as much as he likes. Soon he'll pull up, because he's panting and sweating. Then go and pat him, talk to him, let him hear the sound of your voice; keep in his good books. You need his willingness all the time. Let him gallop the other way if he wants, and do this for an hour or so each day, until he gets hold of the idea of working for his living. It's a thing some of us, horses included, don't take to all that easy.

Next, you want to give him the idea of working with other horses, so find a strong and trusty horse to put with him, and tie him up on the side of the young 'un. Now it's a bit tricky, because he's got the old one on his left side, and you've got him still on a line. He'll jump and buck a bit, and the important thing is to restrain him with the long rope, so that although he can kick and rear you don't give him enough rope to get around in front of the other one. You get a rare bit of confusion once that happens. Don't let it.

Still, the most important thing is the young horse you're

training. He's got to find out what he's there for, to work with others. Start the old horse, and the young one will probably hang back, then rear; never mind, keep your own head, and don't let him have too much of his. Once he starts going then, if you carry on being gentle, you'll find you've won that battle. Turn him and walk and turn and walk, keeping him at it. Best thing to do then it to keep him without the old horse but put him to a set of chain harrows. He can't hurt himself in the grass field. Yoke him properly, and maybe you can do without a false line, which is a long piece of leather with a chain and a snaphook at one end, a buckle round the other which goes on his bearing rein, and the other end fastened back on the other horse's traces. When he jumps, the false line will pull him back. This can be dangerous for the young horse; he may cut his tongue. There's an alternative; have two men near him, one each side, with a long rope, just to steady him. Never mind him jumping, he's bound to do that. Just keep him under gentle control, and let him go anywhere in the grass field. Just keep him going, and give him about two hours. This isn't cruel, not if you're careful enough. And when you take him off, be quiet, talk to him; any animal with a tiny scrap of sense likes to be talked to, and a good horse has got a hell of a lot more than a tiny scrap, believe me. Keep him tied to the other horse while you take him up to the stable; then take him in, take his gear off, give him some feed and some water, and repeat that sort of treatment for a week or two. Let him learn at his own pace. When you think he's all right so far, and is on his way towards doing half a day's work, then the next thing he's got to get used to is working in shafts.

This is where you use a flat roll, a simple implement with a pair of shafts. This is better to start him on for shaft work, because if he decided to be tricky he could be off with a cart and lose you, but with the flat roll he won't run very far. It's not necessary to work him with blinkers; a horse can do without them and never needs them if he is well trained.

Don't let your trainee be put into the shafts in, say, the stackyard. Let another horse bring the roll into the grass field. Put the shafts up vertical. Your trainee horse should be breeched and saddled, two men each side of him, then lead him round so that he stands between the shafts. Gently pull the shafts down, so that the back chain fits in the little ridge on his saddle; do it quietly. Then put on both shoulder chains, then the breeching chains. You need a comfortable thick bit of rope for a belly-band, so that if he balks the shafts won't go up above his head. Let it just touch his belly, not tightly.

Your two men each side are still there. You ask them if they're satisfied with fitting, girths and so on. Then call your horse by his name. Maybe he won't start; maybe he'll try to jump and gallop, and this is where you must hold him tight, all five of you. He's like a child learning his alphabet, and you mustn't crowd him with rules and regulations. So then he's learning who's master, and you can walk him round, letting him get the feel of the shafts.

Lead him, with your hand close to the bit, give him as much variety with the shafts as you can, and probably you'll find two hours quite enough for this. You might find it more than enough for yourself. Then free him from the roll, take his gear off steadily; unyoke, take off breeching chain, then belly-band, then shoulder chains off. And when you are sure that your assistants have done everything, raise the shafts gently, talk to him, take him to the stables, see him fed and watered, talk to him. One warning: if your men haven't got all the gear off him, he'll get a fright when the rising shafts go up, with some of his gear caught, and then you'll have undone a week's work. Caution, kindness, method, kindness, good gear and good men to help, and kindness again, these are the rules for *training* a horse. There's no such thing as 'breaking'.

CHAPTER EIGHT

Cat in the Night

I got my first look at Tab, as she was later called, when I was in the chaff house trying to keep the rats down, which is something a farm's always trying to do and never succeeding. At least, I reckon that when old Charlie Burrows died, that was the time the rats started to win. Old Charlie was a mole specialist (his missis had a real moleskin coat, and Charlie used to say that she prayed for sharp winter weather so that she could wear it to church) and he was pretty good with rats and mice and such like. Well, in that chaff house, ill-lit and no electric, I was fed up. In a quiet second I heard a rustling above my head. I stepped back to try and get a look at the top of the bales. There she was, a finely striped grey and black tabby, long whiskers, a good head and — she was snarling at me at the time — one of the finest sets of cat teeth I'd ever seen.

'Who are you, then?' I asked her.

'PhhhhhhhhhhhhT!'

'Gone feral, have you?'

She cursed me again.

'Keep your fur on,' I told her. 'Nobody's going to hurt you.'

Next time I was in the chaff house, I found three dead rats; cat-killed, I thought, not dog. I threw them on the muckheap and went back into the chaff house. I got level with the top of the bales, and made a tweeting noise. I was standing on a trestle and it wobbled a bit so I grabbed at the top of the bale to steady myself. At once a darkish figure darted forward and before I could jump down I'd had the backs of both my hands scratched good and proper. When I reached the floor I looked up, and there she was, standing on the edge of the bale and hissing like a snake.

'You're a wild 'un,' I thought. 'Can stand up for yourself, too.'

I didn't feel any resentment, though. She was doing what she thought best. I was pleased about the rats. Trouble is, of course, that while you're killing three of the damn things the local colonies are producing three hundred more.

I said to the bailiff, 'We got another, I see.'

'Tabby.'

'Ah, you seen her.'

'Soon have kits, by the look of her.'

I went to the kitchen at the back of the farmhouse to talk with Mrs Truss. Mrs T. was a tiny woman, five foot nothing, but she was dynamo driven.

'Cat? Another? Soon be a blummin' cat farm, way we're going. Mind out, I got more to think about then cats!'

She banged a few more pots and pans about, just to keep me waiting and in my place. I knew the form. This was one of the kindest women alive.

She said, 'What sort is she?'

'Got a head and a tail and a leg in each corner. Oh, she's got fur too.'

Mrs T. put down a pan and looked at me carefully. 'Ain't you got no work?'

'You find something what ought to be done by me and ain't, you can talk. Sorry you got no time for the cat, Mrs T. I'd ha' thought better o' you.'

Her face softened. 'What does she look like?'

'Tabby,' I said. 'Nicely marked, and she nicely marked me too.' I showed her my scratches and she chuckled.

'You got a dish to put her some scraps on?' I asked. 'And then a spare saucer for the milk. We ought to look after her.'

She found me what I wanted. 'Soft you are, Frank Moore. Through and through soft.'

I thanked her, took the dish of scraps and some milk for the saucer. I put them on a bale a bit lower than the one the cat was on. I made a tweeting noise, and there was a faint stirring from the top of the bale.

Tab had three plump kittens four days after she came to live with us. I heard 'em squeaking one evening when I was leaving her something to eat. Daring (I remembered how quick she was with her claws), I stood on the old trestle and looked. I spotted her as she raised her head; she made a rich purr, maybe to show me she bore no grudge.

We didn't go prodding into the mother's private life; I (or young Cecil) used to put her in some milk and meat scraps every night. The kits sounded as though they were getting on all right, and she wasn't scary or unusual in any way, until one day she met Boxer.

Now Boxer was a big black tom, flat-headed, evil green eyes; he had bits of fur torn off here and there in fights, and half one ear gone. He had a stealthy sort of walk, and always looked as though he had a grudge against the whole world; I knew he was on poor terms with Mrs Truss, who had hoofed him out of her kitchen so many times that at last he'd got the message. He was a good ratcatcher, though; that was why he was still alive. When he saw Tab slipping out of the chaff house he stopped and growled, more a dog noise than cat. I came along just in time to see them meet. Boxer circled, keeping his eyes on her, getting nearer and nearer. On his second circuit I saw that he'd a raw slash at the back of his neck. Boxer did all the hissing and provocating; Tab watched him, turning slowly as he circled, but the noises she made were gentle, it seemed to me. Soon, Boxer left off growling too, as though he wanted to listen to her.

Boxer was still; Tab finished speaking. Then she walked up to him and, instead of there being a whirling, scratchy fury, he stood still, and let Tab lick his wounds for him. I've never seen anything like it before or since.

So the animals, other cats included, accepted Tab for what she was and what she did. For the humans, I'll say that she was a tough and determined ratter who regularly laid out four, five or six rats as her contribution to the farm's prosperity. She was distant in her manner; no rubbing and purring, not yet.

When her kits were fourteen days old I felt that I ought to go and have a look; I wondered, for one thing, how she was going to get them down from the bale, which was only a couple of feet from the roof. Cats have been known to take big leaps with a kit in the mouth; I decided to see if I could give her a series of easy leaps from one bale to another a bit lower. I climbed up, and made tweeting noises at her, and wondered how I should show her the way down. I realized that all I'd have to do, really, was to make the steps and leave the rest to her.

Tab wasn't figuring that way at all. She saw me, came to the edge of the bale, looked at me, and rustled away. A moment later she returned with a kit in her mouth, which she deposited on the edge of the bale; and then she stood looking at me. I didn't need a ton of wheat to fall on me. I did what I thought she wanted. I took gentle hold of the wriggling kit, watching her to see if this was right. She just stood. I lifted the little creature gently, and put it on some straw. When I came up again, she was waiting with another, and then the third. Finally, she jumped down and rejoined her little family, one black, one black and tabby, and one mixed tabby like her own colours.

The next time I saw her, she had her three youngsters in an old cardboard box in a corner of the farm kitchen. She was in the lap of luxury, with a bit of old blanket at the bottom of the box, and plenty of room to move around. The kits were playful, and they chased a piece of string I had; Tab wasn't with them.

'Well, that's very nice and comfortable I'm sure, Mrs T.'

'Huh,' she said, 'the little devils'll soon be out of that box, and under my feet all the time.'

'It's a way cats have. If they're so much trouble, who invited them in here in the first place?'

She banged a few pots and pans about, and gave me a searing glare.

I was just moving out when young Cecil stopped me. Young lad he was, about seventeen, full name Arbuthnot Cecil Brown. A tough lad. The village he came from, with a name like that, you *had* to be tough. But he wasn't looking tough now; he looked proper bewildered.

'Mr Moore, you seen that cat lately?'

Before I could reply, Tab herself supplied the answer by

coming in and crossing the stone flagged floor, then she jumped into the box with the kits.

'There she is, then,' Cecil said. Keen lad, wanted to work with horses, as obliging as the day is long. He stared at her, went over and looked down at her. 'There. Marvellous, that was. Never seen anything like it before, what she did.'

'Did what?'

'There was this bullock,' Cecil said, still staring hard down at Tab, 'and he'd slashed himself on some barbed wire. Cat went up to him and started to lick the torn leg. He let her. What do you make of it, Mr Moore?'

'What I make of it, young Cecil,' I said, not being sharp, just suggesting, 'is that you could go and be getting on with some work.'

After he'd gone, Mrs Truss and I faced each other. 'Got any opinions, Mrs T?'

'What I think,' she said, after a bit of silence, 'is that it might well pay us to look after that cat.'

Rumour travels fast in the country; although it has farther to travel than in the town, the lines of communication being a bit stretched, on the other hand it has to pass from fewer mouths to fewer ears. But the amount of embellishment a yarn can get makes you gape in wonder. In less than a fortnight we heard that Tab had killed Boxer, had turned the milk sour, had produced six-legged kittens, had bitten a cow, and had been identified as a witch's familiar that hadn't been seen in the parish for the last two hundred years.

Spider and I were having a drink in the Mucky Duck, served at a steady and far-too-slow pace by Old Sam Gollings, who was retiring soon. Spider queried, 'She's just a normal cat, then?'

'I told you,' I said, 'she's just a wanderer who came into our place to bring up her kittens. She's a good ratter, and she's still a bit stand-offish, even though she does know us all now. She's wild, but not a real wild cat, of course. Just a domestic one gone feral.'

Spider nodded, and paid for our two pints. 'I know. Real wild cats never will tame. Still, Cecil did say that the bullock's leg healed perfect.'

'Cecil should keep his trap shut and concentrate on his job. He's got one now, and I hope to God I was right in leaving him to it.'

'What job this time o' night, Skimpy?'

'Mare foaling any time now. He insisted that he could do the job but I said no and he was to phone me here when she gave first signs.'

'Keen, is he?'

'Good lad, got a lot of book knowledge. He'll make a real farmworker one day soon.'

'There's still something remarkable about that cat, though.'

'You're as bad as any of 'em,' I said. 'You've got to have a bit of rumour to keep you going.'

'There's something in it, though.'

I didn't say anything. I finished my beer and started to move away from the bar. I walked out into the October night, and ran slap into O'Flaherty, one of the Irish lads we employed. The Irish lads worked hard; some lodged in the village, while the less sober variety lived in at the farm, sharing a big dormitory hut on the far side of the kitchen garden.

'Whup!' said Paddy as we connected, and he staggered and I stopped him from falling. He was full of beer right up to the eyeballs, and enjoying every minute of it. He peered at me, trying to get me in focus in the dusk light. 'F-Frank, me old darlin', you're as welcome as a shamrock in November!'

'Where've you been?'

'Boozin',' Paddy said, then laughed like a drain at his own cleverness.

'I can smell that,' I said, 'easy enough. You going back to the farm?'

'Yup,' belched Paddy. 'Ah,' he muttered, 'I'm only beer drunk. That's nothin'. Guiness d-drunk, now, that has a d-d-different flavour entirely. Red Lion, Spalding. White Hart . . . s'all right. Me influ-influ-flential friends'll look after me.' Then he lurched, stumbled and fell, rolled over on the cobbles and lay flat on his back, roaring, quite suddenly, with sentimental songs.

I went round the back of the pub, filled a bucket at an outside tap, and came round to Paddy, who was still letting rip. I threw the water at Paddy's singing head.

'Get up,' I said, 'and I'll see you back to the farm.' I hauled him up, and he swayed like a sapling in a gale. 'I've got to go up there,' I said, 'to relieve young Cecil.'

Paddy nodded wisely. 'Ah,' he said, 'in that case, you being as drunk as y'are, I'd better see you there. Come on, me boy.'

It was no good arguing, so I got him over the stile, which was a bit of a feat, I thought, and we travelled the field path. I got him to the sleeping hut, put him on his bed, and then went to where a light showed in the stables.

I slowed up as I got near to the stable door and peered in quietly. Cecil had finished cleaning down the mare, and was carefully giving her filly foal the once over. The foal bag was stretched on the floor for checking purposes, the afterbirth ready for disposal. No doubt, now, that Cecil was a horse man. It was a real text-book pro job. Foal was feeding too.

I came in. 'Good lad,' I said. 'All by yourself, eh?'

When Cecil looked at me he seemed a bit scared. I could imagine he felt a bit shaky; after all, it was his first delivery. He seemed relieved and frightened at one and the same time.

He said, 'Frank, I've had a fright.'

'Didn't stop you doing what you was here for,' I said, pleased and showing it. 'I know how you feel, lad.' Mother and foal were both a hundred per cent. I saw his face, 'What's up, Cecil? This job's first class. What's the matter? You graduated tonight, boy, you know that?'

He sort of looked past me, very tense. 'Got to tell you,' he muttered, 'got to. You see, just before she started the foal, she was restless, kicking. I couldn't leave and phone you; that's what I should have done, I kept telling that to myself, but I couldn't leave her.'

'Look Cecil. You could have shouted for someone at the farm. They'd ha' been sure to hear. But what are you worried about? You used your own judgement.'

'I had to stay. She was dilatin' early, and I had to check the foal's position; it seemed all right, but she didn't seem to want to shift it. She'd got all the signs, but I was real puzzled. Felt gutsy too.'

'Well,' I said, 'all right. But you dealt with it.'

'Frank, it wasn't only me. All of a sudden I stopped being scared; I couldn't think why. I was calm, real calm, for the time that it was in here. . . .'

'It? What are you talking about?'

'Can we go outside and have a fag?'

'Come on,' I said. We went out into the yard. The moon was full in a clear sky, and a light wind rustled about us. I gave Cecil his smoke.

'It was that cat, Tab. The one who had her kittens here. She just strolled in, looked at me. Never saw such eyes on a cat, so big.'

'Always are, at night, cat's eyes.'

'If you ain't gonna listen,' Cecil said, in a sudden spit of nervous anger, 'then I ain't gonna tell yer.'

'Calm down,' I said. I was guessing.

'Well, Tab came in, purring. She inspected everything, sniffed around. Then she walked round the mare, rubbed against her, licked her here and there. Then she went out, still purring. As soon as she'd gone the mare started the foal quite easy, never had no pain, nothing. That cat, Frank, is something more than we know.'

'Ah. I've been thinking that for some time. Can't say anything definite though, can we?' I looked at my watch. 'Nearly eleven o'clock, boy. Off you go, I'll see her comfortable for the night. Tell the employer about you tomorrow.'

Cecil sighed a deep sigh of relief. He ground out his fag with care. 'We'll see the cat in the morning, eh?'

'We'll not learn anything,' I said, 'but I reckon we'll see her.'

But we didn't. Tab and her three kittens had gone forever. Don't ask me how she could manage with that little family to guard and feed, because I don't know, unless it could be some power we can only guess at. I just hope that, wherever she calls next, she'll get the same sort of reception we gave her. Maybe, as Mrs Truss said, there *is* an explanation – but we'll never find it.

CHAPTER NINE

And Forgive us our Trespasses

When I was a boy we had a parson named Ernest Archibald Brayley. That was when the verger used to thump half-a-dozen choirboys after the service because they mucked up the Lord's Prayer by joining in and, at the right time, raising their voices and saying, solemnly, 'give us this day our Brayley dead.'

Why should I have remembered that on this sunny October morning from all those years ago? Could be, I thought, as I turned up past the Mucky Duck towards Long Main Woods, because the wife and I had had a few words, and sharpish, just after breakfast. It was nothing, nothing at all; it was just that she was a bit sensitive about a remark I passed about the crust of the last pie she made not being up to her standard. She had said, 'You wait, Frank Moore. I'll remember what you said about my pies.'

'It's not *pies*, Evelyn, it's pie. That particular one. Any of us can make a mistake. Any of us. And a fall from Grace don't seem so bad when you climb back into it again, does it?'

She looked at me very steady. 'I've got a funny feeling,' she said, 'that I might do without your company for a bit.'

'How about two and a half hours?'

'What for?'

'Go up to Long Main, take a sack for firewood, half a pint at the Duck, back here at half-past twelve.'

She thought about this. Then an idea seemed to strike her. 'Yes,' she said, 'that'd be about right. Yes. In at half-past twelve. One of these days, my lad, I'll make you eat your words. You stick to horses and leave the pies to me.'

'I only said —' but then she was gone, and so I got an old sack and walked up to Long Main thinking odd thoughts, like I said, and letting time go by that easy I didn't know I was walking, and all the time the sounds and smells and sights of the country I love were chucking themselves at me, free and without the asking.

In the woods I was soon into Long Main, looking for bits and pieces. There were notices 'Trespassers Will Be Prosecuted' but that was only for strangers. His lordship (only he wasn't a lordship, just a common everyday sir) was a liberal-minded sort of man, and he was regarded with respect and some little admiration in our part of the world. I never remember him prosecuting anybody; he was a gaffer, but he didn't trouble us any.

Neither, for that matter, did his head man, Joe Seckley, a lean wiry fellow quite a bit older than I was, but very light on his feet, and in his way a perfectionist. Nobody ever looked after pheasant and partridge chicks the way Joe did, no one was better at

snaring and at keeping down vermin, and nobody knew better
how to temper justice with mercy. It was Joe who sat up four
nights running defending that badger sett, when some clowns
from over Terrington Marsh way thought that they'd do some
hunting with their terriers. Three nights passed, and the fourth
night they came and found themselves looking down the barrel of
Joe's shotgun. It was his 'illegal' shotgun, too. A repeater of five
or six cartridges, continental make of some sort. They thought
Joe wouldn't shoot, but he did, and took half a yard of bark off a
tree not four foot away from the nearest of 'em.

'Get out,' Joe said, quiet as ever, 'and stay out. Next time
you'll get a dose of lead poisoning. Out.'

They went. That was the time when Joe ran a pet badger, and
a nicer creature you couldn't wish to meet. It used to amuse us to
see all the village dogs learn their lesson that Buster was to be left
alone.

'Stand still, you!' snapped a voice behind me. I heard
footsteps. 'Put your hands up.' I did. Then I heard a chuckle and
I turned round.

'Damn me, Joe, you had me fooled,' I said, and we laughed
together.

Joe nodded at my sack. 'Hook and crook?'

'That's right,' I said, 'should be a few fallen branches after this
week's winds.'

'Do you a bit better than that,' Joe said. 'They're thinning out
top end some time next week, and I'll see that there's some bits
and pieces over for you. I'll get one of the boys to collect 'em, and
drop a bag in for you at home.'

Joe was a quiet bloke with steadfast eyes, never unhappy,
though I believe he often thought of how sad his wife had been —
a sort of permanent cloud as you might say — when their two boys

were killed. He was a man who'd got big resources deep in him, not a man to be put off from doing what was right, regardless.

'Thanks, Joe,' I said.

As we walked, I thought I heard some other rustles from behind us. I hesitated once, then stopped and turned round. Joe turned too.

'Joe,' I said, 'am I seeing things?'

Not three yards away from us were two of the biggest cock pheasants I'd ever seen; I'll swear their tails were nearly four foot long, and they stood looking at us as though we weren't dangerous to 'em at all.

'Well, damn me,' Joe said, but not angrily, just exasperated. 'It's Mutt and Jeff turned up again.' He shook his head, grinned, and put a hand in his jacket pocket, then bent low and held out a handful of corn. These two pheasants stalked up and fed from him as though it was the most natural thing in the world.

'You're well in with these two, Joe,' I said. 'Finest birds I ever saw.'

'They're a blooming bother to me,' Joe said. 'I reared 'em, see, from chicks; they know me all right. But first shoot we had these two flew straight towards me and landed at my feet. Protection. I couldn't shoot 'em, now, could I?' Then we both saw the funny side of it and laughed, and because the corn was finished Mutt and Jeff left, proud and shining.

'Got some nice old bits of branches here and there,' Joe said, as we walked on. 'Don't miss 'em.' He pointed where the leaves had drifted. I soon had a fair load in the sack, more than enough.

Joe said, 'Frank, can you give me a few minutes, and come along a bit further?'

'Course,' I said. 'What's it about?'

'Tadge.'

'What's he been up to now?'

'I reckon,' Joe said, as we left the track and rustled through the leaves, 'that he's had a bad spell of some sort. I can't imagine what goes on in that poor fellow's head; sometimes he's easy to talk to, and other times, well, he just stares past you.'

'You asked parson's opinion?'

'No. And I ain't going to. Parson'd want to see the poor fellow put in a home. That'd be no good to Tadge.'

'He'd die,' I said, and after that there was nothing more to say until we reached the clearing where, deep in the wood Tadge had his home. It was a slung-together sort of place, with bits and pieces of wood and plank and corrugated iron, and with a rain butt and a chimney sticking through the roof at a crazy angle.

We stood and looked. 'Never seen his place before, have you, Frank?'

'Not this one,' I said. And I tried to imagine Tadge in there, and what it was like in the depths of winter.

'Lives on what he can catch, or scrounge,' Joe said, 'but he's one o' God's creatures just the same. Reckon he must ha' been behind the door when they were dishing out common sense. This is the only life he knows, and I reckon that if he was turned out of here, he'd die.' Then Joe walked towards the hut with me at his side. 'Don't look to your left, just keep on looking at the rain butt.' I could only just hear his voice.

'Why?' I wanted to know.

'He's watching us,' Joe said. 'He often does on Sunday mornings, waits until I'm gone. Come on.'

We went inside. It smelled damp, but not all that unclean, and I just stared round and wondered what it was that brought a man to this. Under the plank and straw mattress bed there was a cocoa tin. Joe picked it up, and it rattled. Inside was a shilling and a few coppers. Joe took two half-crowns from his pocket, and dropped them in the tin.

'You do that regular?' I asked.

'Somebody has to,' Joe said. His face wrinkled like a smiling walnut.

'Here,' I said, 'he can have this,' and I put in one beside Joe's two. After all, what did missing a call at the pub matter?

Evelyn said: 'You're a bit on the early side. It'll be ten minutes, yet.'

'Where's the kids?' I asked her, picking up the dear old *News of the World*.

'They'll be here,' Evelyn said. 'They can tell the time. They'll come home starving as usual.'

I read the paper for a bit; I thought of talking to the missis about Tadge and Joe. Then I thought how good the food smelled, and I went into the kitchen to wash my hands at the sink.

I could feel Evelyn's eyes tickling the small of my back.

'Smells good,' I said as I hung up the towel. 'What have we got on, then?'

She looked straight at me. 'We've got,' said my dear wife, speaking very clearly, 'we've got steak and kidney pie; then we've got apple pie, and then if you're still hungry you can have a slice of mincemeat pasty. Pastry,' she said, severely, 'what's as good as any you'll taste in the four corners of the kingdom. Anybody as finds my whole morning's work "below standard" can have a go at it next Sunday all on their own.'

I'd just managed to give her a kiss when the kids arrived, shouting to be fed.

We never used to talk much at mealtimes, anyway, but on this Sunday all you could hear was the champing of jaws and teeth.

My missis asked a question with her eyebrows. I answered it with the thumbs up sign, and I thought about Tadge and gave thanks. For all I know, the Almighty could well have put something on the credit side of my account.

CHAPTER TEN

Fire and Bellows

In our scattered village in South Lincolnshire we had a very old-established family, the Tates. What I mean is, while we Moores were what Snodger Waite used to call 'A-similated', the Tates had been there when Wykely Castle had been a going concern. There were two branches of this family, sometimes called 'Wheel Tates' and 'Blacksmith Tates', though the truth of the matter was that they could all of 'em have come out of the same mould. They were all thin and strong men, the sort who eat like horses at every meal and still stay as thin as rakes.

One afternoon, early April it was, I'd knocked off work a bit earlier in order to see if Elias could do something about a couple of scythe blades I'd just taken out of the grease and didn't like the look of. Walking into that forge was like walking into a living museum, with the great fire and bellows, the bits and pieces hanging on the old grimy walls, the stores of fresh lengths of iron and steel, and the acrid smoke and clang and noise.

Elias and his large young striker Henry Wattis were in the middle of a really artistic job, with bending patterns, great hooklike sets of pliers and so on.

''Lo, Frank,' Elias said.

'Gates?' I asked.

'Yeah.' Elias stopped work for a moment. 'Joe came and ordered 'em for Sir Eustace. Going into that little wall he's had built across the rock garden.'

I admired the nearly completed one. 'Going to look good,' I said. 'Where do you find all the patterns, Elias?'

'They come to me,' Elias said, 'and when I've worked 'em out, people are usually satisfied. People don't know what they want in this line, so you have to show 'em what they want.'

'And if they don't like 'em?'

'Then I do 'em another one,' Elias Tate said, 'until they're satisfied.'

He meant it, too.

Somebody walked in beside me and I didn't turn for a moment. I asked Elias, 'How many dissatisfied customers have you had since you've been in business?'

Elias pushed his mucky old cap, decorated with blue goggles, back onto his head. He took the question seriously, and Henry Wattis stayed for a moment to listen.

'There's some old diaries and papers we've got tucked away in the house,' he said, 'so I can answer that. There was a gent in 1791 what got a bit ratty because the gates he ordered were the wrong size. They had a bit of a stack-up over that, so I'm told, because he supplied the measurements for the things. That taught us a lesson; we don't take anybody's word, now. We always measure ourselves.' He looked past me. 'What can I do for you, Joe?'

Joe Seckley carried a fearsome looking leather sheath, about 2 feet long. He nodded at me. 'Afternoon, Frank. If we'd known we were both coming here somebody could ha' saved a journey.'

'Can you make these last another year, Elias?' I handed him the scythe blades. Elias stood in a shaft of sunlight, carefully thumbing the blades, squinting down 'em, thumbing them again.

'Just about,' he said. 'Nice bit o' steel you got there.' He turned to Henry, now standing near the fire like a patient ox. 'You come to a full stop, Henry?'

'I have,' Henry said, 'and shall do until you've finished. Job for two here.'

'What've you got there, Joe?' I asked.

He took it from the leather sheath. It was like a long chopper, heavy. 'Mashet,' Joe said. 'Here.'

I fingered it. 'Heavy. You get a swing at something with that, and something's got to give.'

'That's right. Just a tool. Picked it up at an auction at Gedney. I fancied it. Might come in well for a bit of rough hedging. Anyway, it's one for the collection.' He took it from me and handed it back to Elias. 'Can you fine the blade down a bit, so she takes a good edge.'

Elias grinned. Some school kiddies peered into the dark Aladdin's cave of the smithy. Elias said, 'What you mean is, you want her for an outsize razor.' He addressed me. 'He should ha' been a blacksmith. Keeps tools in condition better than any other man I know. Your private collection, eh? Leave 'un with me.'

And Henry Wattis, an urgent sort of young fellow for one of his size, started to blow up the fire again as a hint for everyone to get out and let Elias and himself get on with the work.

One April evening I was walking home; a shower had just stopped, and I walked thinking of nothing much except what a smell good earth is after rain, and how soon my own early taters would be showing. I saw Elias coming towards me. 'Afternoon Elias,' I said.

He turned his head away, and never spoke. I turned to see him walk on, head hanging down a bit, for all the world like a beaten dog.

When I got to the forge clouds of dust were billowing out. I stopped and squinted inside, just as Henry Wattis peered out, him being I supposed the source of the clangs and thumps and muck-raising generally.

'Cleaning up a bit?' I said, obvious, but cheerful.

Henry came clear of the fug; his face was black and the expression under it was pretty dark too. 'Bloody am,' said Henry, and went back into the gloom again, where I could hear him chucking large bits of this and that about. I followed him in.

'I just met Elias and —'

'Met Elias? You got no pleasure out o' that, I'll allow. Hey up, I gotta move this.' He picked up a bundle of iron pieces, slung them aside like a bundle of faggots, and began to sweep along the wall corner where it hadn't been swept, at a guess, for about a hundred years. A couple of wandering hens got the cloud of dust right at 'em. They hopped it, clucking.

'Slack time?' I asked, still chatty.

Henry scowled at me from a distance of about six inches. 'No, it ain't slack time. You know it ain't.'

'All right, what's going on?'

'Frank, some men are as ununderstandable as wimmen. We got work and enough, what with Elias still wanting to keep his farrier jobs. I shall leave. I've tried everything, straight I have; nothing else for it. It's not natural. Worse than a lovesick girl. He'll make himself ill. Me, I reckon he's ill already.' Then he came out into the sunshine.

'Come here,' Henry said, 'round the back; got something to show you. I reckon you ought to rouse public opinion about this. Pride. Pride? I never heard aught like it.'

We were in the yard. Under the lean-to there was an old wagon wheel, sturdy still, but with a section of the circumference missing and the old iron tyre beside it. 'That effing thing,' Henry said. 'That's what done it. That.'

'That made him – upset? How?'

'I tell you,' Henry said, 'the whole bloody human race lives in total ignorance about what its next-door neighbour's like.'

I was missing out on a vital point, that I knew. 'Well, it's a wagon wheel needing repair.'

Henry lit a fag as though hoping it would explode in his face. 'It's more than that. It's a disgrace, it's heartbreaking, it's a catastrophe.'

I just listened.

Henry said, 'That there wheel is more than forty years old. It's carried God knows how much overloading.'

'Things break and wear out.'

'I know it,' Henry said, 'and you know it. Any fool knows that, any fool except Elias Tate.' Young Zac Tate, skinny and blackhaired, came through the yard.

'Seen me dad, Henry?'

'Seen enough of him,' Henry said.

'Elias is no fool,' I reminded Henry.

'He usen't to be, but he is now. Now he acts like a kid what gets whipped for stealing apples, forgot to say his prayers, or got a girl in the family, or something.' Henry lowered his voice, and thus showed his real concern for his employer. 'He's in disgrace, that's what. That a wheel made by Tate's wore out. God's truth, that's it!'

'You mean he's down in the dumps because . . .' Henry meant it. 'Well, I'm damned.'

'He's the one who feels damned,' Henry Wattis said. 'If you and me had had a pound for every time that wheel turned in its life, we'd not be here. I wouldn't, I'd be living it up in Wisbech.'

I'd never thought of Wisbech as a place right suited for living it up.

'Says he'll never live it down.'

I never suspected that Elias could think like that. I knew that every job he did was right, I knew that he'd get on with a job any time he was asked, I knew that he never filled out any overtime for himself or any of his family; I knew, too, that in young Henry Wattis he'd got somebody who'd stand by him; no matter what Henry said he himself would do, I was sure that Henry was loyal, even if he didn't have the huge pride the Tates had, pride which was like an iceberg, nine-tenths hidden.

'You know, Frank,' Henry said, 'he'd take notice of you. You're steady, if you don't mind me saying so. You and a few others could help him. Convince him. Talk to him. Talk to him and get him drunk. Anything, so long as he listens. He needs — er —' Henry thought a bit, 'he needs therapy.'

'Therapy, in a pint pot?'

'That's right.'

'I've seen Elias drink twelve pints and then walk home sober,' I said. 'Wouldn't it be cheaper to call in the vet?'

Henry looked hurt. 'Now, you know what I mean. Show him he has friends, show him we don't give a hoot for the bloke who made the wheel that only lasted forty years, but we do care about him. That's the programme.'

'Who'll get him there?'

Henry flexed his muscles and his grimy shirt just about took the strain. 'I will,' Henry said, 'even if I have to carry the silly old sod.'

On the night we'd fixed for Elias Tate's rehabilitation, I walked into the Mucky Duck fairly early, so that I could prime anybody who didn't know what we were going to do. I told old Sam Gollings behind the bar and he mentioned it to all who came in. There was a man sitting in a corner with a whisky in front of him. That marked him out as a foreigner at once; at the Duck they sold only a bottle of whisky a month, except around Christmas time. I ordered a pint, then took another look at this man. Then I saw that it was Tommy Egerton, who used to go to the village school with me long back in the time we lived near Market Harborough. We were pleased to see each other, no error.

'Been chasing you round, Frank. Missed you at home, at the farm too. Have a whisky?'

'Beer,' I said. 'I'm strictly a beer man.' I looked him over. 'Looking prosperous, Tommy.'

That seemed to tickle him. 'Frank, I'm a union secretary. How the hell can I be prosperous?'

I asked him what union and he told me.

'Do you like the job?' I asked.

'Sometimes. And then again sometimes I have to remind myself what the real idea was behind unions being organized in the first place. Then I get mad over those dolts who never come to meetings and then organize unofficial strikes. Expect the executive to rubber-stamp everything they do.'

'Learned to keep your temper, have you Tommy?'

He knew what I meant, and laughed. 'I've learned. But it still comes hard at times.'

The bar was gradually filling up. Elias Tate hadn't shown up yet; maybe Henry would have to carry out his threat. I didn't doubt that he'd get Elias here by force if it were necessary.

'I had a blow-up at a meeting a couple of weeks ago,' Tommy said. 'Lost my temper good and proper. Shouldn't have done, couldn't help it though. I hollered "stop calling me and everybody else brother! We're here for one reason only", says I, "and that's to sell our labour for the best price we can get. Anything else is a waste of time and downright hypocrisy!" One old fool asked me if I was calling him a hypocrite, and I said yes I was. That shut him up.'

I offered Tommy a whisky, but he said no he'd have a beer with me. And when we were steadily getting down these, I told him about Elias Tate and the wheel that wasn't good enough.

'Frank, you're pulling my leg.'

'I'm not.'

Tommy laughed, with not much real laughter. 'All right, I'll believe you. But I'll bet I couldn't tell it to any of my mob. Pride in craftsmanship, responsibility, duties before rights. . . . You can't use that kind of talk nowadays, it just don't work. Today they'll split hairs over who drills a hole in what.'

I said, 'There's still a bit of the old craftsmanship here. Do you know, I can go into Gedney and buy handmade sheepskin gloves for ten bob a pair?'

Tommy nodded. 'This Elias Tate. What sort of a man is he?'

'Not the over-cheerful sort,' I said. 'Not bubbling over, as you might say. What he needs is telling that he's got friends; he's that cut up about it —'

The door opened and Elias came in. We got a pint down him quick. We chatted heartily, and young Orb Philimore sat down at the yellow-fanged piano and played 'To be a Farmer's Boy',

'Nellie Dean' and still, without his left hand knowing what his right was doing, did us his special, a bit of 'Colonel Bogey' for which tune he had as fine a set of dirty words as was ever hollered out in a public bar anywhere.

Nobody mentioned the wheel, but everybody was chatty and cheerful, and, after his tenth pint, Elias did look as though he was thawing out a bit, and thinking maybe that life was still worth living. We kept two games of darts going, and made sure that Elias was supplied with beer (straight, I don't know where he put it; must have had hollow legs) so that at about his fifteenth pint he was getting just a bit mellow.

But still there was one thing we hadn't planned, and that was going to outdo all the good we were trying to do. After about two hours, when Elias was outside in the gents, Joe Seckley came in, his face like a thin old walnut, with a large grin and a piece of wood under his arm. He said his hellos, got himself a pint and then asked, 'Where's Elias?'

'Here,' Elias said, coming back into the bar.

'Got your new glasses, yet, Elias?'

Elias didn't know what Joe meant. Joe heaved the piece of wood at him. 'Catch!'

Elias caught it. We all stopped, just watching.

'Need your glasses, don't you?' Joe said.

'Eh?'

'What was your father's name, Elias?'

'Zacharias.' He handled the wheel spoke as though it were suddenly more than hand hot.

'Look at the back of it,' Joe said, 'turn it over, Elias, and tell us what it says there.'

Elias got himself focused. 'Reuben T.' he read. 'Reuben. That was grandfather Tate!'

'So it was,' Joe Seckley said. 'Can remember him when I was a nipper. That wheel's over sixty years old, and now the tyre wears through for the first time. What do you want to give people, Elias? Eternity?'

It was a happy evening, after all. I walked part of the way home with Joe Seckley. It was a dark, mild sort of night and we were leisurely. Suddenly Joe stopped, took something out of his keeper's bag and slung it over a hedge.

'Joe,' I said, 'what was that?'

'Never you mind,' Joe said and chuckled.

'That wheel spoke?'

He never answered.

'It was, wasn't it?'

'It was,' Joe said.

'With his grandfather's name on it.'

'That's right. I checked on the wheel, and there it was, so it wasn't too difficult to convince Elias, especially as he wanted to be convinced.'

We walked about another fifty yards. Then I said, 'Was the name there, or did you put it there?'

'What do you want?' Joe asked me, 'a happy ending or a bloody argument?'

A few days later I was coming by the forge just as Elias and three helpers were lifting the new wheel tyre from the circular fire all ready to seat her round the wooden wheel, and then douse her cold so that she gripped tight. When they'd finished I caught young Henry's eye. He came over.

'He repaired it, then?' I said.

Henry shook his head. He was a bit awe-struck I reckon. 'No, not really. He made a new wheel, same as the old one, ready for maybe another sixty years' work. No charge.'

'No charge. Well, dang me.'

'He says that if a man don't honour his responsibilities he might just as well be dead.'

CHAPTER ELEVEN

A Policeman's Lot

A policeman who is posted to a country area has a lot to learn. He has to learn that regulations have to be interpreted, stretched a bit this way, shoved a bit that way, in order for rural life to go on the way it should; above all, he has to be shown that the most vital set of police procedures as applied to country life is that elastic lot of deeds, misdeeds and near-misdeeds which is known to the policeman as The Ways And Means Act.

Our new copper (this might have been 1931 or '32) was a big, cheerful young fellow named William Figgis. He came from Lincoln, was earnest about his job, and friendly in a very slightly nervous sort of way at first. He was unmarried and found lodgings with two elderly ladies, the Misses Walker in Copley Drove.

You couldn't help liking Bill, and I used to feel sorry for him when he had to realize that regulations for swine fever and slaughtering, fowl pest or sheep dipping could all be awkward when you met them in real life. He had to inspect horses if they had shoulder sores or there was ill-treatment suspected.

Being the new copper, he was under scrutiny from everybody around our scattered village. He was never refused help, because it was soon quite clear that, even though he was as green as a field of spring corn, he was a trier; he was willing, he was pleasant. In his first few months with us he had all sorts of initiations, from pigs about to farrow to the fact that Tadge was a vagrant and ought to be left that way, aswell as the fact that in our area the kids were apple scrumpers by both instinct and training and could lick him for speed any time they wanted. Credit due to the lad, he tried to see that through, going to see Mr Paston, head of the 'tin-top' school, to ask for the names of boys who were dishing out apples to their mates at morning break. That was until the kids got wise and sat on the apple hoard until it wasn't hot any longer.

P.C. Figgis had only a bicycle to help out with his duties. He never got used to the distances he was supposed to cover on the little criss-cross back roads round our farms, but he kept at it, learning all the time. He consulted me more than once about animal management questions which bothered him, but soon he had all the help he wanted from anybody in the area. But he could still be caught unawares.

I remember the time when I worked for an employer who had two farms. Coppice, the larger one, was where most of the workers lived, as well as the employer himself, and then there was Seabank Farm, so named because that's where the farm was, right on the edge of the sea except for the ridge of the big dyke that kept it safe from flooding. I was horse man now, but at harvest time you worked anything up to twelve hours a day, and everybody had to give a hand. All your horses had to work harder too. If the man driving the binder was a big fat 'un, that was fine, because the weight was balanced out. Me being skinny, I always used a lump of rock that weighed about three stone and that made it about right. But one of the horses, one normally stabled at Seabank, got something far worse than a shoulder sore, and I was a bit wild that whoever was responsible for it had let it get so far established. Young Orb Philimore had this horse; his parents, heaven help us, had christened him Aubrey, and he wasn't a bad lad by any means. He was known for the way in which he kept several girls on the trot at the same time because he had a little Velocette motor bike. He was also known for the cockroach racing he organized at the back of the Mucky Duck on Sunday mornings. Many a dinner has dried in the oven when the man who should have eaten it was betting his money at the back of the Mucky Duck. It was easy, with a lookout, to dodge the attentions of the police, because all you had to do to be clear of suspicion was to tip the cockroaches, racing box and all, over the wall of the pub, and then all come out by the gents as though you'd been out for natural reasons.

'You know what that horse's got?' I asked him.

'No, Mister Moore. Didn't see it. Mr Waite never said. He had it the week previous, I reckon.'

'Anybody who could have missed this,' I said, 'must be either blind or an idiot.'

Orb said carefully, wiping the sweat from his neck, 'I don't reckon he is blind.'

I fished in my pocket and took out a little roll bag which I always carried with me. It contained an old but very sharp razor and the biggest pair of tweezers I've ever seen.

'What is it?' Orb asked. He was a bit irked, I think, at doing nothing with all the harvest work going on around him in that burning sun which had given us such a fine harvest that year.

It was certainly nasty. The flesh around the thing was discoloured for about a nine-inch patch, and when I shaved it down to the skin it looked worse with the red inflamed centre holding what looked like the dirty, inflamed top of a mucky little carrot. I touched it and the horse twitched uneasily.

'That's a fistula, my lad,' I said, 'and it's got to come out now, and this horse put out of service for a week or so.'

'Guv'nor won't like it,' Orb said.

'He'd like it a lot less if he had one himself.' I said. 'This has got to be seen to.'

'Looks nasty, Frank,' said our copper, who had just arrived. He slung his bike at the hedge and hung his helmet and uniform jacket over it.

I'm not fond of spectators when I'm horse doctoring, but I didn't say anything.

Bill Figgis saw what I was doing. 'Septic?'

'Stinking,' I said. 'Got to get it out. Hold his head,' I said to Orb. I started to go round the edge with the razor, easing the filthy thing, and Orb made sounds to the horse to soothe him and tell him to take it easy. The horse did so.

'There,' I said, 'that's as loose as it'll come, I reckon. He all right, Orb?'

'Yer.'

I opened up the tweezers almost as wide as they would go and got a firm grip. 'Now,' I said, and out it came, like a little stubby carrot, stinking of putrefaction.

'Great,' Orb said.

Bill Figgis didn't say anything. I buried it, and then turned to look for our copper. He was by the hedge being sick.

I'm not saying that Bill Figgis was perfect, or that he didn't make many more blunders in learning to be a country copper. The fact is he made some imperial-size clangers in his first year or two with us, but any criticisms weren't serious when we'd got to know him a bit. He was a man who could make a decision and act on it when it was necessary, and when he clearly understood what was the trouble. There was the time when little Cindy Lewis, who should have been walked home by her elder brother, fell into a dyke and was nearly drowned. Bill fished her out and took her home. He found home locked up, so he broke in and cleaned up the child and got her comfortable and read her a fairy story into the bargain. He also collared the elder brother and gave him a talking to, and when Griff Lewis came home and learned about his daughter's accident and his son's sin of omission, Bill Figgis left hurriedly so as not to interfere with the criminal assault that Father Lewis was about to unleash on his shiftless son.

Bill, in addition to everything else, was learning to take a joke against himself; he grasped the idea that our kind of fun wasn't often cruel, and never to people we liked. But still, there was one episode which he never lived down. It's the sober truth that the biggest trick ever played on Bill was not done by a human, but by a pig.

It was a sharp, clear night in October, and Bill was cycling along one of the scores of little droves and lanes which cross and recross the fen over thousands of acres. It was getting on for midnight, which meant to him that all good citizens should be in bed. He was interested to see a couple of lights on at Crockett's. Someone went across the yard with a hurricane lantern. He'd never visited Crockett's before, and now seemed as good a time as any to make the call. He walked his bike into the yard, and a kennelled dog growled at him. He crossed the yard to where a light shone from a window, and knocked.

Old man Crockett peered out. He was seventy, a good farmer in his own little way.

'Who's that?'

'Mr Crockett?'

When Bill stepped in the old chap saw who it was.

'I just wondered if you were all right, Mr Crockett? The light being on –'

Old Crockett, who looked as though he'd not slept for a couple of days, shook his head. 'I'm all right. Bit short o' sleep. 'Part from that, I ain't worryin' about meself.' He jerked his head to the interior. 'Worried about she.'

'She?'

'Come and look.'

Bill went to look and saw the biggest sow ever lying on straw, grunting and snuffing. He didn't know what to say, quite, as his only previous acquaintance with pigs had been sausages and pork chops. 'She's big, Mr Craddock.'

'Ah, she is, that.'

'She ill?'

'Dang it, boy, 'course she ain't. But her piglets should ha' been here two days ago, 'cording to my figurin'. She ent started yet, so I get no sleep. Can't leave her, you know.'

Bill agreed, though he wasn't clear why a sow couldn't be left to carry on with farrowing. But he did know that old Crockett was just about all in. So, kindly, he offered to relieve the farmer for a bit.

'You go and have a rest, Mr Craddock,' he suggested. 'I'll keep an eye on her for you.'

'You will? Ah, you're a good lad. Ain't met you before, but I heard good on you.'

'You go and have a rest,' Bill said. 'I'll stand by here.'

The old chap pottered off gratefully, and Bill sat and watched the uneasy, distended bag of flesh on the straw. After a short while, he began to nod.

He was roused by the sudden grunting and gasping of the sow, and he looked up just in time to see the first pig born. As just about anybody (but not Bill Figgis) knows, when a sow farrows the piglets leave her and then walk round to her head as she lies there. You have to take each one as she produces it, and stop it from this natural intention. She'll be paining at least until all the litter's out, and if you don't get 'em first she'll eat 'em.

So, Bill Figgis saw the little piglet come out, and it worked its way round to the mother's head. One crunch, and the little creature was eaten. P.C. Figgis had never seen anything like it.

A few minutes later the same thing happened again, the new piglet going round to its mother's head and being swallowed in a couple of gollops. Bill was fascinated.

She did it again. Bill scratched his head and thought it very rum. Just then old Crockett came in.

'How is it, then, boy?' he asked.

Before Bill could reply another piglet was born, scuffled round to the mother's head, and was gone in a couple of good chomps.

'Oh, my life!' cried old Crockett. 'Oh, deary deary me, look at that, look at it! Did you see what happened?'

'Now, Mr Crockett,' Bill said. 'Don't get alarmed. It ain't anything to worry about. I've seen the little bugger do that trick four times already!'

CHAPTER TWELVE

The Little People and Others

—

I

Ted Roberts was the most quietly happy fellow I ever knew. Even great pleasure only raised a nod of approval and a smile, but the smile went all the way through; it wasn't ever just a surface effort, for politeness. Ted was a really lean fellow, leaner than I am, and about four inches taller. He was quiet about everything he did, and he chose his clothes so that when he stopped he just seemed to melt into whatever background was there.

I went out with him early one morning. He wanted to have another go at landing one or two of the big chub that lurked under a backwater bridge. Louts, these chub were, with strong ideas about territorial rights. When I'm finished with this life, one of the pictures of earth I'd like to take with me is the glow of that early summer morning, the grass heavy with dew, and the sun's flat rays sending night off into hiding.

We didn't talk much. We had our tackle, and we could both of us walk miles and never feel a bit tired. We passed over the backwater bridge, and stopped a bit upstream. Ted lay down his rod and took from his satchel something wrapped up in a couple of handkerchiefs. It looked like what might have been a pie crust. When he'd got it undone I saw that that was just what it was. He gestured with it at me, for a moment, with a faint smile, and then he broke it up and scattered it over the water.

'Wakin' 'em up, Ted?'

He answered me without looking away from what he was doing. 'They been awake hours,' he said.

'The pastry —' I began, and then I shut up; I had that feeling that I was trespassing on something private.

He said, quite simply, 'The pastry is for the kelpie.'

Again I was just on the point of making a useless remark, but stopped myself, while watching Ted continue to break the pastry.

I watched a kingfisher whip low across the stream like bright blue lightning. And I still waited.

Quietly, watching the fragments float away, Ted told me, 'My missus makes fine pastry.'

'How often do you do this, Ted?' I was careful, like a man trying not to scare off a couple of feeding deer.

'Once a week. Regular; seems to be right time.'

'Oh,' I said.

'Did you know this stretch of water, ten years ago?'

'No.'

'It's changed,' he dusted off his hands. 'Down there, in the water. Was near pollution level. Now it's very nearly drinkable.'

'And there's more fish than there was ten years ago?'

'Oh, yes.' He had found his pipe, and was filling it with care. 'All for the sake of a little pastry offering about once a week.'

'Who told you about the – er– kelpie, Ted?'

'Gypsy.'

'When?'

'About ten years ago.'

'And you fed the kelpie all that time?'

'Not quite true, there. It's an offering to the kelpie. He should see it given, that's the important thing. I'm beholden to him.'

'What made, I mean what got the gypsy talking about this? Was it a real gypsy?'

'Ah, she was. Genuine. About twenty, I reckon. Camp up by Long Main. Child had wandered, cut a leg on some barbed wire. I found the child – little boy – and I washed his leg and bandaged him. Missis did, rather.' He looked very straightly at me, now. 'Child's mother came to fetch him, though nobody had told her what happened.'

'You mean that she just came and found you?'

'That's what it looked like. After she saw what we'd done, she told us about a neglected kelpie in this river. She said that if I honoured him once a week, and we tried a bit of re-stocking, then all would be well. And it has been, just like she said.'

'Ah,' I said, and watched the water. I didn't have to tell Ted that I believed him, because he knew that I did. To show any disbelief of such a story would have counted as an insult.

We had heard that Nan, Ted's wife, was ill for hospital. If you're ill for a medicine (castor oil, for example), that's one thing; if you're ill for the doctor that's another; but ill for hospital's *serious*.

I looked in by making a wide detour on the way home, and I

arrived just as the ambulance was taking Nan away. Ted stood there like a lost child waiting to be rescued.

'Hospital,' he said.

'I heard, so I looked in.'

'Thanks.'

'How ill is she, Ted?'

Ted managed a twitch of a smile. 'It's biggish, but it ain't malignant.'

'Ah.'

'Doctor says she's a strong woman. So she is, mind and body both.'

'Straightforward case, then.'

'Hope so.'

I said, 'Ted, while Nan's in hospital, you come and stay with us. We've one little room spare, with a bed. Come and stay.'

He looked astonished. 'I couldn't do that. Do you know the time I get up, some mornings?'

'I work with horses. I am an early riser, too. We could be up about the same time. Evelyn'll fix some snap for us, and we can have main meal together about half-past five or six. Suit you?'

Ted agreed. The system worked, and we got nothing but good news from the hospital. Young Orb took Ted to visit her on Sundays, and that was proof that Ted loved his Nan very deeply. What I mean is, one ride on young Orb's bike was enough to scare the hell out of you, but Ted stuck it and he was glad.

But a week after he'd been with us, I got a worried feeling, and didn't know why until I'd chased it into a corner and made it give itself up.

Pastry. The Kelpie. I'd no idea how long it would take for the water guardian to get a bit hufty through neglect, and I'd no idea how long Ted's Nan would be in hospital.

So one morning I got up early and Evelyn was shocked. I can remember her now, with her bonneted curlers and an expression of disbelief.

'What's bitten you, Frank?'

'Nothing.'

She picked up the alarm clock and rattled it, put it down and stared at me. 'Do you know what the time is?'

'Time you was asleep,' I said and off I went.

That evening, we all had a meal, all except baby Horace, and he wasn't in chewing shape, yet. There was a sort of a strain over the whole business – eating, I mean – but men as hungry as we were didn't have time to notice.

'And now,' Evelyn said, 'we'll have the apple pie.'

Ted looked past me, as he often did when he was thinking. I looked past the missis, as I occasionally do when I don't want her to see what I'm thinking. She came in and plinked the apple pie dish on the table. But it wasn't a pie, it was just cooked apple.

I reckon that for a few seconds we must have looked as still and as glassy eyed as some of the statue groups in Madame Tussaud's. I could feel my missis' stare burning my ear'ole. Ted saw the crustless pie. He looked at me, at Evelyn's thunder and lightning expression and then back at me again, and slowly a smile creased his face.

'Never, Frank. You never did!'

My dear wife was nearly at boiling point, and she was right, because I only had to ask her to make some pastry and she would. I knew all that; it was just that I thought of the thing and did it, without any ifs or buts. I grinned at Ted. 'I did.'

'You just snuck off early and –'

'I couldn't stand the risk of you being called a thief, could I?'

Ted laughed.

'Now look here —' my missis began.

I laughed and said, 'You wouldn't understand.'

'Oh wouldn't I? What does it look like, a pie with no crust?'

'Drat my Sunday bowler woman,' I said. 'Ted's the one who understands *best*!'

She said, 'You'll be the one who makes the next pie crust, if you're not careful!'

'Thank heaven,' Ted said, 'my missis'll be out of hospital before that has to happen.'

Then we all laughed. But Evelyn didn't take to this story. 'My goodness,' she said, 'old wives' tales!'

'Missis,' Ted said, 'if that's what you believe, I'll give you a challenge. You go along to the old black bridge at midnight, stand there and say, while the village clock is striking:

> Kelpie of the winding river,
> I no more will be your giver;
> I do not want you close to me,
> So Kelpie, off you go to sea.'

Evelyn laughed. Then she added, 'Suppose I did say I'd go?' Ted became serious. He said, 'You wouldn't get there to do it.'

'Why not?'

'Because,' Ted said, quiet as ever, 'I'd stop you.'

She looked at Ted for a long moment. 'All right,' she said, 'he's your kelpie. Let's leave it.'

II

Being in the horse-doctoring business as well as working daily
with the beautiful creatures, I often had contact with the gypsies.
With their brightly painted caravans and their own language,
they were a race apart, but a friendly race, I found. And I tell you
this, I've been to some funerals in my time, but never a one
impressed me as much as did the true gypsy ceremony I saw once
on the common ground near Long Main woods, with the
beautiful caravan burning, cracking and fizzy in a rising and
falling sea of prayer all round.

I learned a bit about horses, too, by talking with them. My
father hobbled up one day and saw me putting ordinary grate
blacking on a shoulder sore.

'Where'd you get that one from, boy?'

'Gypsy.'

He thought about it, trying to remember what there was in
blacklead that made it good for sores. At last he said: 'Oh well,
main thing is that you can get on wi' 'em.'

He grinned. 'They say same about you now as they used to say
about me — friend of the gypsies with a bit of the Old Man in
him.'

The employer kept a roster of those next for any emergency duty,
and as this was agreed on by both Coppice and Seabank farms,
then there was no argument. We were short of chaff, and we had
to have it. Dick, the man who had the steam engine, was behind
schedule because of a breakdown the week before. It took him
eight days to get the spares and two hours to put the machine
right. And he told the employer that it was Saturday lunchtime
or not at all. He wasn't being nasty, just a hard-working man

stating plain fact. And who was elected? Yours truly, and the little bloke from Seabank Farm.

We met up at Coppice, and exchanged hello's in a wary sort of way.

'Saturday bloody afternoon,' he said. 'I ask yer!'

The engine was chuffing along the poplar avenue to Coppice. Dick steered her in, and stopped his exact belt's length away from the chaff cutter. Dick was a thick, red-faced man with black hair, and not in the best of tempers.

''Sup wi' you then, Snodger?'

Arthur Waite gave him look for look. 'Naught as'd interest you.'

Dick dropped down to the ground and stood a foot taller than Snodger. 'Summat's got you, you old sod. Wassup?'

Snodger sort of hunched himself up. He glared. 'You done make me work Saturday afternoon.'

'Don't talk soft,' I said, 'you and me was next on the roster.'

'Look,' Dick said. 'With the backlog of work I've got, it's now or never. Emergency. Ain't that right, Frank?'

'Don't ask me to control him,' I said. 'One word from me and he does as he likes.'

Snodger Waite didn't move.

Dick looked a lot but he didn't say any more. He hauled out the belt, and I put it on the engine fly-wheel and the chaffbox wheel.

And Snodger, a short, wispy little chap, with annoyance reddening his face, still didn't move.

Dick barked at him. 'Well, are you workin' or not? It's buggered my Saturday we well as yourn, you know that?'

Snodger finished staring at the steam engine. 'Oh,' he said,

'I'll work. I mean *I'll* work. But I tell you for nothing what *won't* work.'

Dick showed his teeth. 'Well?'

'That belt.'

Dick and I stared at the belt. I walked to it to see if there was a flaw Snodger had seen and I hadn't. It looked all right to me.

Snodger said, 'That belt won't stay on. You see, it won't. It'll be coming off the whole time, and there's nothing you'll be able to do about it.'

'I been driving this engine twenty year.'

'Drive it forty, it don't matter. That belt won't stay on.'

'That look all right to you, Frank?'

I said it did.

'I'll start her up then.'

Snodger just grinned, evil-like.

You can believe me or not, but if that driving belt came off once it came off a hundred times. We tightened it, we slackened it, and shifted things around, thinking that maybe some unevenness in the ground was the trouble. But it wasn't. We tried an old spare that Dick carried with him, and that was no improvement. The afternoon grew grey with thickening cloud, and rain would soon be with us, and still that belt kept coming off. Dick and I walked about with grim expressions.

Snodger stood there, hands on hips. 'Wunt get no beer now,' he said. 'Bill Figgis has been round the back for his pint, and it's all shut up.'

'I wish you bloody would,' Dick said. He looked like a man who, as my father would have said, was going to have his rage any minute now. I was feeling less than pleasant too.

Snodger stood back and surveyed the scene. He grinned. 'Ah well,' he said, 'I reckon we can get on with it now, eh? Made my point, didn't I?' Dick's expression was fit to skewer him to the ground. 'She wunt come off no more. Let's get on.'

And from that moment, until we'd finished the job, the driving belt ran straight as a dye; not a flap or a wobble.

Young Windlestone-Fyffe, the lad who was supposed to be learning to be a farmer and his father paying damn nearly as much as he did to send the young dud to Eton, strolled by. 'Everything going on all right, you chaps?'

Snodger grinned and said yes, but Dick and I just turned and looked at him, and he backed off and said he'd see us later.

When we'd done, we started to clear up. Snodger left first because he'd a fair walk to Seabank. The rain which had started as a drizzle increased. I sheltered with Dick under the engine tarpaulin.

Dick looked after Snodger. 'I've heard of such things, but I never thought I'd have one done to me.'

CHAPTER THIRTEEN

Exchange is No Robbery

Before the incident of the steam engine belt I'd never seen anyone with 'a touch of the old man' in action. Never before, and of all unlikely people, Snodger Waite was the unlikeliest. But having seen it, I noticed now the way he was greeted by gypsies passing through. Now, with much time passed, I remember how it used to be said that when there was a heavy downpour, Snodger was a man who could walk home dry. I never saw that, but I did see that maybe his 'touch' was a bit of a compensation for the life he had to lead. I never felt scared of him, this reed-voiced little fellow with spaniel eyes. He had a lot to put up with, did Snodger, with his five kids and his missis and living out at Seabank.

Windlestone-Fyffe, our farm pupil, was another oddity, but he didn't have a touch of the old man; five and more years at Eton had knocked any magic pretences out of his head, along with any sense he might have had before he went there. He lodged in the village with a widow woman and her daughter.

But Windlestone-Fyffe, called 'Tusky' because he had the finest set of air-cooled teeth we'd ever seen, used to love to play lord of the manor.

One day I was down at Seabank Farm, helping with some ploughing. It was high breezy, and the noise of the wind played a duet with the crash of the waves the other side of the big bank. Snodger counted as second horse man there, and Sid Dennis was number one. Their two cottages could be seen from where we were working.

When we were having something to eat, Snodger asked, 'You fancy a bit o' rat'n'?'

A seagull swooped by and nearly had all my snap in one go. I said, 'You had that kink in that barrel o' your gun straightened yet?'

Snodger scowled. 'We'll need a gun, but I was thinking of my ferret.'

'That's his latest toy,' Sid said.

'Can you handle a ferret for ratting?' I asked.

'He thinks he can,' Sid said.

'I know I can,' Snodger said. 'Bought it off Tusky.'

'Out of your mind,' Sid said.

'How much?' I asked.

'Ten bob.'

'You paid enough, I reckon.'

'You put it in the hutch with the rabbits?' Sid asked him, and he said it so straight-faced that Snodger couldn't tell if he was having his scotch pulled or not.

'Hutch on his own,' Snodger answered. 'A bit fierce, like a good ferret oughter. Bloody near had my finger off.'

Snodger knew that both Sid and I liked ratting, though neither of us was fond of ferrets. We two stopped outside the farm about a hundred yards from Arthur's house. We didn't go any closer, because nobody could be sure how Mrs Waite was feeling. Still, standing there, we got a good indication. The salt breeze wafted her words to us. 'Tek it!' we heard. 'Go on off wi' yer mates an' play, you and your ferret both! Hope it has your hand off! And if you're late for tea you'll have it in cinders, in the oven!'

Snodger came out grinning, his ferret box tucked underneath his arm. 'Missis is in a good mood today,' he said. 'Now, whose crossbar am I riding on?'

'Not mine,' said Sid, 'it ain't safe.'

'What ain't safe about it?'

Sid had his answers. 'You ain't, for a start. Number two, that bloody ferret what's trying to gnaw its way through the box ain't safe. Your rotten old gun what you just forgot ain't safe. Would you say that ferret was A-similated, Frank?'

'Definitely not,' I said. I could hardly keep from laughing as Snodger's face saw the force of the opinions gathering against him.

'Go you back,' Sid told him, 'and get your unsafe gun and your missis's unsafe bike and then we'll say the Lord's Prayer, after which we'll be off, the most un-A-similated hunting party in Lincolnshire.'

'I come from Norfolk,' Snodger said.

'I knew you had summat wrong with you, but me natural politeness stopped me from saying anything. Very reserved, us Lincolnshire men are. Get a move on, will yer?'

The laughter was all the richer to me because there was no malice in it. Snodger didn't mind being kidded, except when it got to the point of somebody taking it for granted that he *was* an idiot.

Anyway, off we went, with Mrs Waite's good wishes (or something) following us out towards the sharp and windy banks. It was a steady push all the way to the ratting ground, but the journey was enlivened by the sight of Snodger who in order to ride his missis's bike had to adopt a praying sort of position because the handlebars had rusted solid and couldn't be adjusted. Also, there was a spring coming loose on the saddle; it could have done him a terrible mischief with every turn of a wheel.

But Snodger chattered away happily. 'Lotsa holes along here. You'll see, I tell yer, you'll see. Adge'll be a fine rat hunter; it's in his blood.'

Sid, pushing steadily, panted rather than asked, 'Who?'

'Adge.'

'Your ferret,' I said, 'that's his name?'

'Adge,' Sid said. 'Chase me to my Aunt Fanny's. What a *name* to give the creature.'

'It's nice and friendly,' Snodger said.

'Which is a sight more than he is, by the looks of things,' Sid told him.

As we approached our hunting ground the banks gave us some protection from the wind.

''E's a killer,' Snodger said, 'that's what he is, eh Adge? A real killer.' And he nattered on like this for some time, trying to work up his blood lust, which was the only kind of lust he could afford, what with having five kids. 'Rarin' to go, ain't you Adge?' And he scratched at the netting and the creature leaped in fury. Snodger laughed. 'Coo, he didn't half give me a dirty look.'

'No he never,' Sid said. 'You had it long before you met him.' The rest of the journey was in silence, because Snodger was working out what Sid meant and the process of trying to think didn't suit him.

We parked the bikes, and walked along at the bottom of the bank; on the other side of the bank the sea sounded as though it was trying to tear the whole thing down. We sploshed our way through puddles and did a detour here and there, and the bank seemed full of the right sort of holes. Snodger was carrying Adge with a firm grip.

At last we stopped. 'Go on,' Sid said, 'set him to work. Let's see your killer in action.'

'Which hole?' Snodger asked.

'Set him down, for Pete's sake, and let him pick one.'

So Snodger put down the ferret and it sat and blinked. Snodger made a wary snatch, picked it up, and put it about three foot away. No reaction.

'You're sure he don't want a pair o' glasses, Arthur?' Sid asked.

'Give him time,' Snodger said.

'Not A-similated, maybe,' I said.

'Give him time.'

I looked at this ferret closely. 'He wouldn't bloody move if you lit a fire under him.'

Snodger looked at his ten bob killer and then at me. No countryman likes to think he's been done.

'Arthur,' I asked, 'you fed him?'

''Course I have,' Snodger said, a bit irritable. 'I don't want him to die. Had to argue over him with the missis. I sold her the idea that it was a good investment.'

'Reckon she'd sooner have had a new hat,' said Sid.

I had to explain to Snodger. 'Arthur,' I said, 'you'll never get a well-fed ferret to work for you. No appetite, no incentive. It'd sooner have a nap in front of the fire, like any sensible animal.'

'You for instance,' Sid said.

'Ah,' Snodger said. 'Ah, righto. He'll not warm his whiskers in front of my fire, until he's done some work. No work, no eat.'

'You mean no eat, then some work, then eat.'

Snodger accepted the idea. Then he stared hard at us both, and got narked because he could see we were fit to burst out laughing.

'What I think is,' Snodger said, 'that if he ain't the killer he's supposed to be, then young Tusky will be asked to pay back me ten bob.'

Sid hadn't done with Snodger yet. ''Course,' he said, with his face straight as a lath, 'maybe the animal's cross-bred.'

Snodger fell for it, though he was getting a bit heated by now. 'Cross between what and what?'

'Can't be certain,' Sid replied, 'but I reckon that it was a dead secret between his mother and a couple of buck rabbits.'

The meeting between Snodger and Windlestone-Fyffe took place on the following Tuesday in the Mucky Duck. Sid Dennis had just whacked Snodger and me at darts. Ferrets hadn't been mentioned, and all was calm and peaceful.

Then Windlestone-Fyffe made his appearance, bid everybody good evening and bought himself a pint. Turning round with it he got jogged by Snodger.

'Ah, Mr Waite. Do have a drink.'

'Thanks,' Snodger said, 'a pint please.'

The pint appeared and Windlestone-Fyffe paid. 'And how is Fortescue, Mr Waite?' He saw me. 'Ah, Mr Moore. You'd like a pint, wouldn't you?'

I said I would, and thanks.

'And how is Fortescue?' he repeated.

'Eh?'

'The ferret, my dear sir. I trust he's flourishing?'

Snodger having accepted Windlestone-Fyffe's hospitality, found it cramped his style a bit.

'How is the dear little chap?'

'Er – ah – some might say he was all right.'

'Oh, hasn't he settled down? Perhaps the change of scenery has upset him a bit. He'll be all right.'

Conversation in the bar had subsided; no one wanted to miss this bit.

'He'd better settle down,' Snodger said, 'and soon. Ten bob I paid you for him.'

'Certainly, and not an exorbitant price, so they tell me.' He searched Snodger's face with good will. 'Nothing wrong, I hope?'

Snodger started to open his mouth, but this time I got in first. 'He thinks there is because he tried to work the ferret just after feeding him.'

Windlestone-Fyffe nodded, concerned. 'Oh yes, he has to be in the right mood, you know. And that starts with how much there is in his stomach.'

'How many ferrets you got?'

'Five,' said Windlestone-Fyffe, 'now that Fortescue is with you.'

'I call him Adge,' Snodger said, firmly. Beer was served and paid for in whispers. Snodger, known for shooting his mouth off, was now being out-classed by one hundred per cent politeness.

'Fortescue, or Adge as you call him, was the smartest of the lot, in many respects,' said the learner-farmer.

'And you sold him to me.'

'Yes, Mr Waite, that is so. I fail to see –'

'If he was the smartest of the lot,' Snodger said, 'why sell him to me?'

'If I remember rightly, Mr Waite, you asked me to sell him to you and offered ten shillings.'

We enjoyed it all, every word.

'Yer,' Snodger said, and I could see that he was feeling cornered.

'So really,' Windlestone-Fyffe said, 'you got what you asked for.'

Henry Wattis suddenly exploded into laughter in the middle of a gulp of beer, and sprayed the room in a fifteen foot half-circle.

'What I wanna know is,' Snodger said doggedly, 'is why you sold him to me if he's so bloody good?'

It occurred to me that there was one occupation that would have suited Windlestone-Fyffe down to the ground. He should have been an MP. 'My dear fellow, the reason is simple. I have only limited accommodation for the ferrets, and I had to dispose of Fortescue because he was (a) too ferocious, and (b) much too randy for any form of ferret community life. You really should be well satisfied with such a fine animal.'

Snodger was turning pink, going on red.

'Told him,' Sid Dennis said, 'that he didn't give the ferret a proper chance last Saturday.'

Snodger fixed his eyes upon Windlestone-Fyffe. 'I might want to change that ferret for another.'

Windlestone-Fyffe was cool. 'Bargains made should always be bargains kept,' he said.

'You mean you *wunt* change him?'

Windlestone-Fyffe beamed pleasantly. '*Caveat emptor*, old man,' he said, and left the bar. A rumble of amusement and approval followed him, and the bar took up its usual volume of chat.

'Had you there, Arthur,' Sid said. 'Ferret's all right. It's the chap what owns him ain't treating him right.'

'I'll treat him right,' Snodger said, 'I'll treat him good and proper. When I'm done wi' that animal, he'll catch half-a-dozen rats before breakfast, and like it!'

The end of the following week, we were all three ploughing in the nearest Seabank farm field to the sea. We could see Sid's and Arthur's cottages, right down to the bottom of the garden where the hutches were. A newish looking hutch contained Adge. And I thought that Adge was going out of his mind, if he had a mind to go out of. Every time I saw Adge he was tearing up and down his cage and clawing at the wire. I said to Snodger, 'That ferret.'

'What about him?'

'Acts a bit peculiar, don't he?'

Snodger grinned; it was the sort of grin that might mean shame in some and downright cunning in others. 'You'll see, Frank, he'll work next Saturday. If he don't, it'll be the worse for him.'

On Saturday afternoon Sid and I arrived to find Arthur had Adge, and his rotten old shotgun with a kink in the barrel. He also had that bike of his wife's which could well have been safe for a female only.

Nevertheless and notwithstanding, our Snodger seemed in good spirits. 'Cold, innit?' he said as we got going, 'all them old rats'll be at home, won't they, waiting for old Adge here to chase 'em out, ain't they, Adge?'

'Watch where yer goin',' Sid growled.

'You're very happy, Arthur,' I said.

'Am,' Snodger said, 'can't lose either way.'

'What are the two ways, then?'

He grinned. 'You'll see.' To Snodger, A. Waite Esquire was the smartest fellow he knew.

We parked our bikes and made our way along the land side of

the bank. The wind had freshened, and water from the breakers was spilling right over.

Snodger stopped and pointed. 'There,' he said, then he stepped into a puddle, and nearly dropped Adge. He considered the situation. 'Now, if I put him in here, you should be able to shoot the rats as they come out.'

Sid took the gun, and stepped back a bit. Snodger put the ferret down. We waited for action, but nothing happened. Arthur gave the ferret a nudge with his boot, a wild look beginning to creep into his eyes.

'So where's all the blood lust?' Sid asked.

Then we got action. The ferret found a pool of water and began to drink from it. I winked at Sid; Arthur seemed flabbergasted. Sid sat down first, and then Snodger and I sat down, Snodger on the bank, just above the ferret, and I with Sid on the other side.

The ferret kept on drinking; the level of the water dropped an inch down from when he'd started. The longer he went on drinking the more amazed Sid and I became, while Arthur sat there with a face like a homeless thundercloud.

'Driest ferret I ever saw,' Sid remarked.

Adge went on, lap, lap, lap.

'Gimme that gun,' Snodger said.

We gave him back his gun. 'See a rat, Arthur?'

'Keep yer still.'

The ferret went on drinking. I tried to edge round a bit to see if there was a rat, but Snodger only said, 'Keep yer still.'

The damn ferret never looked up. It went on drinking like a Scot on Burns' Night.

Then Snodger took aim. I couldn't see what his target was, but whatever it was, it was pretty close to the ferret; at that range, the shot would whip out almost in a solid lump.

It still looked as though he was going to shoot, though the ferret was the only animal in sight. We waited. Bang!

When the smoke cleared we saw bits of ferret scattered about the marsh grass, five or six yards.

'Arthur,' I asked him, 'what the hell did you go and do that for?'

Snodger gave me that look which showed that he knew that Sid and I weren't up to his standard of brain power. 'Told you, dint I?'

'All you've done,' Sid said, 'is to see your damn ferret blown to kingdom come. Some of us, Arthur, ain't as green as we're cabbage-looking.'

'True,' Snodger admitted, 'very true. Like when Tusky Windlestone-Fyffe thinks he's pulled a fast one on me, him and his ferrets and his blood lust and keeping 'em hungry and whatnot. It's a yarn, a tale. That'll show him!'

Sid raised his voice. 'What the hell are you goin' on about? You just killed your ferret, dint you? Then you're ten bob down!'

'Ain't!' said Snodger.

'You are!'

As Snodger rose to his feet his righteous indignation rose with him. 'You may think I'm daft, Sid Dennis, but I ain't. I snuck around his place three nights ago, and got this one.' He nodded at the scattered evidence. 'Just wanted to see if what he said was true. It ain't. I've proved it, haven't I?'

At that moment my mind gave a little twitch, like it does sometimes when I'm dealing with animals. 'Arthur,' I said, gently, 'what did you do with the first ferret you had?'

Snodger looked at me pityingly. 'Huh. I fooled him proper. He'll never find out. I've done him proper, see. When I snuck up there I changed that first ferret for the one I had this afternoon!'

He smiled at us, lofty as a short man can get, while words, hot, searing, blasting words rose in my mind. I judged that Sid felt about the same. He said quietly, 'Let's all go home and have some tea, eh?' I just nodded. We prepared to go.

'You goin'?' Snodger asked.

'We are,' Sid said, 'before one of us loses his temper and kicks your arse-bone through the top of your hat!'

CHAPTER FOURTEEN

A Dip in the Briny

Despite the fact that we sometimes got so ratty with Arthur
Waite that we could willingly have bound and gagged him and
chucked him into the creek, we always made allowances for him:
we knew that he was a genuine eccentric, and ought to be
preserved, like, say, Lincoln Cathedral. Snodger was an original.
Snodger being a man of surprises, seemed to affect the balance
(just a very little) of all who knew him, and I reckon that our
lives were the richer for it.

One hot, July day, Peterborough show week hot, we were
ploughing in a second crop of clover at Seabank Farm. Three of
us, Snodger, Sid Dennis and myself were on this job, and we kept
hard at it, and we could see that we'd have it licked in about a
couple of hours so we took a rest.

Snodger, who was bright pink and sweating like a squeezed
sponge, squatted down and wiped his face. Sid was one of those
who get brown at the first touch of sun in April. Me, I was
reddish.

'Ennit the limit,' Snodger said. He wasn't asking, he was telling.

'Bloody is,' Sid agreed.

'I'd give a pound to be able to dive into ten foot of water,' I said.

Snodger looked at the dykes and creeks of the sea. 'We ain't short of water.'

When the tide was in there were whole areas covered in sea water. When the tide was out only the larger and deeper channels had water in them. It was a longish way to walk, but right then I just wanted to cool off.

Snodger said, 'The old long 'un'd be a good place.' He pointed it out. We'd be all right there if we got to it just before low water. The creek was about an acre in size, and about ten feet deep, so Snodger reckoned. It was near the windmill pump, the one which was always chucking back water without ever seeming to catch up with its work.

Snodger said, 'Come yer back t'night when yer turned y'horses out, then we'll goo t' that'n over there.'

I had my tea, told Evelyn where I was going, and went and put on my bathing costume under my clothes. I collected Sid Dennis, and we went along to Snodger's.

'Is he ready?' I asked Sid.

I was enlightened as soon as I'd said it. Mrs Gladys Waite was raising her voice. 'Arthur Waite, you're a fool!'

Arthur was taking his life in his hands and answering back.

'Arthur, take it off!'

Mutinous mutterings could be heard.

'Arthur, do you hear me?'

Medium-loud answer from Snodger. 'I can't help 'earin' yer.'

She roared. 'It ain't decent!'

Snodger said: 'They're all right on you.'

'Take 'em off!'

'Ain't gonna!' For a little 'un, Snodger could make a noise when he wanted.

'*Take 'em off!*'

Snodger was now angry and determined. 'I told yer; this is an emergency!'

'Is it? Well, I ain't gonna have you emerge looking like that!'

The Waite's cat shot out of the house.

'Dunno what the fuss is about,' said Sid, 'but we should be getting results any minute now.'

Snodger came out, and we got our first glimpse of what fashionable sea-bathers were wearing this year. Snodger was wearing his boots and socks; on his head he had a battered straw hat with the lid coming loose, like an old salmon tin. The rest of him, from armpits to ankle, was a huge pair of bright green female bloomers; there was room in there for another one beside Snodger. He looked like a reject from the chamber of horrors.

At last Sid and I sobered up a bit, eyes running with tears of laughter, and still bursting with little spasms of mirth. Snodger stood there in all his glory, complete with his missis's bike.

'You ain't never going out like that, Arthur?'

'Bloody am.'

Mrs Waite came to the door and the trumpets of battle resounded again. 'Booby!' she announced, and the volume of sound made our ears click. 'Booby! That's what he is! Oughter be certified!'

Snodger tested his wife's bike cautiously to see that none of his drapery caught in the wheels.

'Watch that bike, Arthur,' said Sid, 'it'll have your knackers off in a flash.'

Mrs Waite made one final appeal. *'Are you going to come back in the house and dress decent?'*

'No,' Snodger said. 'I'll do all right like this. Got no pockets to put me matches and bacca in, but I'll manage.'

She slammed the door; Snodger grinned at us. 'See? I got in first with what I wanted to do, and she can't do nothing.' He burst into song. 'Hey, boom, tiddlypush, who's got a horrible mush?'

We set off. The tide was down, and only the main channels, used by boats and barges, were visible. When the water was up, then you couldn't tell if you were stepping into two feet or twelve.

'What time's tide in Arthur?' Sid asked.

''Bout one in the morning,' Snodger said.

As we worked our way through to the place where we were going to swim, I realized that it was a tricky business, and that time was worth watching. We skirted a few water-logged hollows, we went up and down a few banks and found a few slushy corners, and at last we arrived. The evening sun was still hot enough to fry an egg.

Anyway, we got there, and it was a real treat, with nothing in the world more important than having a splash and a swim. We were like boys again. What I mean is, Sid and I were like boys again, but what Snodger looked like with his salmon tin boater and his missis's bright green pair of whatsits, I wouldn't like to have said.

We'd been splashing about and swimming the best part of two hours when I saw a funny sight. I looked at King's Lynn docks way out in the distance, and I looked at a ship coming along from our right, bound for the docks no doubt. From that direction, too, clouds were building up, heavy and leaden.'

I asked Sid what he thought.

'High tide's midnight, I reckon,' he said.

A doubt grew in my mind. 'That boat's *not* going to the docks. It's coming this way.'

A few drops of rain fell.

Snodger said, 'Boat's on the water, rain's in the sky, if we all get under, we'll all keep dry.'

Sid spoke to Snodger with some heat. 'Listen, if that boat's travelling inland, then it's got water to float on, ain't it? We came across from the windmill, didn't we? Orright, you look over that way now!'

'Water's halfway up it,' I said. 'Come on, let's move now. We're a long way from safety.'

Sid addressed Snodger, 'Are you dead certain you can't swim?'

'Not a strike. Why?'

'Because now would be a bloody good time to start learning!'

We started back, working our winding path back to the windmill; after twenty minutes, the thing seemed the same size as before. It was a sickening feeling. We were forced to go a long way round where, before, we had crossed easily, and now the short cuts were becoming awash with the tide. Worst of all, you could never be certain if your next step would put you in deep water. Eventually, just when I was beginning to think that we'd made a fair bit of progress, disaster struck. Snodger, a few yards away from us, said, 'Glup!'

'OhmiGawd!' Sid exclaimed.

'He ain't gone far,' I said; I took my mark from that soppy straw hat floating on the water. I hauled Snodger up to the surface again. He spewed water like a bathing elephant. 'Next time you do that,' I said, 'I'll keep you under! Stay close to us and maybe you'll live!'

We battled on; I don't think I had ever before realized the force of the tide. We found out then, and I reckon each one of us knew that the next fifteen minutes could be his last.

Then there was a diversion. Along came a large rowing boat with two men in it. They drew level with us as we trod warily along a shallow. 'Good evening, gentlemen,' said the elder of the two. I had the idea, I don't know why, that they were both parsons with their collars the wrong way round. One waved a map at us. 'Could you tell us, please, if we can get to Sutton Bridge lighthouse this way?'

We were flabbergasted. There we were, three human beings clearly needing assistance, and all we had was a request for traffic directions! We told them and, unable to speak for fear of the awful profanity which would ensue, we watched them go.

Correction; two of us watched them go. Snodger was away again, and this time it looked as though he was a goner. An eddy brought his soppy straw hat to me; I picked it up and imagined it on top of Snodger's coffin.

Sid was looking out to where the water broadened quite a bit. 'Thinks he's a seal, or something. Can you see that soft ha'porth anywhere, Frank?'

We stared hard. The odd thing at the time was that I kept thinking 'Snodger won't die like this, Snodger won't die like this. . . .'

Then, about half a mile away, a lump of outsize lady's bloomers climbed soggily up a bank, and Snodger was inside 'em.

'You screwy old clod!' Sid roared, 'you frigging noodle, what're you going that way for? Come you back here!'

Snodger started back towards us, and I was still frightened of that tide, and the power that was in it.

'I reckon that was the right way!' Snodger called.

We didn't acknowledge his opinion. 'Sid,' I said, 'somebody's got to be in charge here, or we're all done for. How well do you know the creeks?'

'I don't.'

'I do, just a bit. Follow me?'

Snodger arrived, a green, trembling grampus.

Sid grabbed him. 'We're following Frank from now on, you keep between us.

It was a damp and weary trio which at last climbed to safe ground by the windmill. We found our clothes and bikes. Swallows were dodging bats by the time we arrived at Seabank Farm cottages.

Mrs Snodger came tearing out. 'Oh Arthur, love, Arthur, are you all right?' She clasped him to her generous bosom and Snodger didn't come up for breath for thirty seconds. The little Snodgers gathered round too. Quite a family party. Then, still hugging and crying, they went inside.

'I wonder,' said Sid.

'Wonder what?'

At the very moment a screech from within the house, erupted onto the evening breeze. 'Hey,' she roared, 'hey look at you, you nasty, untidy, careless, little humbug! You ripped my knickers!'

CHAPTER FIFTEEN

A Proper Send-off

I believe I've mentioned that most of the land where we worked was owned by Sir Eustace Tillington Wyke-Brown. We didn't see much of him in person, but his assistant bailiff, Ernie Arnold, assistant to Joe Seckley, was around. Joe liked the gamekeeping part of his bailiff's job the best, and there wasn't any friction either in Coppice Farm, where I spent most of my time, or Seabank. There were other farms around, all belonging to Sir Eustace, and I reckon they were all pretty well run. Coppice, however, was boss farm, and the only one with fair sized woodland and copse. It seemed to make Coppice Farm the natural centre of the work.

It seemed to us, at the time, that there was some sort of stability about life. There were a few 'neighbour quarrels' and sometimes the odd scrap, but no hard feelings. There were a few annoyed grumblings about 'that there headmaster at the tintop school, who couldn't keep a flock of sheep in order even if he had a couple of good dogs working for him'.

So, this evening I was having a pint in the Duck, and sizing up this character from Wisbech what they called 'Monkey' Mostyn. Young Orb was telling me that he had a new motor bike, and I wasn't paying a lot of attention. I was, well, a bit disturbed about something. The bar door opened, and Jimmy Dutton stood there. His friends stood there and said hello, and he didn't say anything. Then he walked to the bar and leaned on it. People came a bit closer, and watched.

Jimmy just stared at the bar.

'Joe,' he said.

'What?'

Jimmy's eyes were scared, and sad. 'Joe Seckley. He just walked into his home, put his gun in the kitchen, sat down and died.'

It was some minutes before we could take it in. Joe with his gun on his arm, thin, cheerful, a face that was nut brown the whole time. A healthier man you couldn't . . .

You could hear how everybody felt in that pub, awkward silence, with the darts players stilled, and nobody drinking. Everyone was forced to realize that a great and good friend could be whipped out of this life away from those he loved without a by-your-leave or word of warning.

Then the murmurs. They ran into each other and overlapped; they were a kind of hymn of praise for Joe, blunt though some of the words were; they were what we felt.

'Joe. Was he in here, last night?'

'Yer. Playing darts, right where you are.' The man addressed moved a foot away.

'What age was he?'

'Sixty-one.'

'No age.'

'And fit too, he was.'

'Never had anything wrong with him in his life.'

'Could have betted Joe would ha' reached ninety, and still be fit enough to walk up here every day for his pint.'

'Rum.'

'Bloody shame, that's what it is. I could draw up a hell of a long list of them as should have gone before Joe.'

Orb called to Jimmy, 'Who's with his wife?'

'Neighbours. Mrs Dykes. They've sent for — they've done what's needed.'

'Doctor?'

'He don't need no doctor. I know a dead man when I see one.' He asked Monkey for a scotch; Jimmy's tears were on his cheeks.

And still the men in the pub talked in soft reverence. They might be lacking in learning, but they were all of good will.

'His Lordship won't get a man in all the five counties to touch Joe.'

'Too true. What Joe didn't know about our work wasn't worth knowing.'

'That's what I liked about him. He'd show anybody how to do any job.'

'And he knew when to turn a blind eye, eh?'

'Yer. Damn good darts player, too.'

Then, as good men will, their talk turned to the one who was everything to him, his Edith.

'She's not destitute, anyway.'

'Wunt be neither, 'long as there's men working on farms round here who knew Joe.'

'Cottage is his.'

'That's a blesing.'

'Not sure that it is.'

'We've all got to help . . .'

The door of the bar opened. There stood Tadge, mucky, ragged, like a lost dog what's been kicked too often. He just stood there, his eyes watering, and grief rising in him like a tide.

'True, ain't it? True?'

If I live to be a hundred and one, I shall never again hear the voice of misery and despair the way it came from Tadge then. He started to say something else, tried again, and stopped, choking.

'Best man in the world,' he managed to say. 'Best man – man in the world –'

Then he stopped, clinging to the doorpost, staring, flowing with tears.

We saw Joe off properly. They were able to make the funeral Saturday afternoon, and I reckon that every farming community for 30 miles around sent someone. He was to have a wagon funeral, and my employer's under-bailiff said we'd better take a day to get ready. The wagon had to be repainted the night before. Young Orb worked with me, getting the four shires cleaned up and fancied. Everybody and anybody who could help did so, and I reckon poor Edith Seckley never knew she had so many friends. She was a quiet little woman whose whole life had centred upon her Joe.

It was a beautiful day; the kind of day for a man to restate his faith, if he can find a way of doing it honestly.

I had thought, rightly or wrongly, that the wagon with its beautiful repaint and the four shires looking ready for a show would be the centre of things, for this was how Joe would have wanted to go. But I soon felt that the really important thing was the great number of people who had come, from Holbeach, Spalding and Peterborough and hundreds of little places, for Joe's last journey. And it was more than just the numbers; there was something else which I felt, and that was all the minds of those people, acting like one and praying for Joe. A man can give a little prayer or thanks any time; I don't exclude the thirsty man who downs his first pint after a long and dusty day and says 'thank God for that'. But I didn't say that to Evelyn; and she didn't say anything about this great turnout until I did.

'I suppose you could say that Edith Seckley's lost everything.'

'Family, you mean?' The people thronged, talking to each other quietly, like a great humming of bees.

'Tom and Ernie —'

'And now Joe.'

Tom and Ernie had been thirty months older than me, twins. The army took them away and then they were killed and, thank you for the use of your sons, missis.

Sir Eustace arrived, got out of his car, and went to talk with Edith Seckley. Now, there was something we liked about him; we knew for certain that he'd cancelled two important conferences to be at Joe's funeral. His chauffeur told us so.

'She's not lost everything,' I said.

Evelyn contradicted me in that soft voice she uses when she's sure I'm wrong, but doesn't want to rub it in.

'She's got friends,' I said, 'plenty.'

'None that loves her,' my wife said, and took hold of my hand.

The church was packed; by Sir Eustace's request, it was to be family first, then fellow workers, then village people. The church just about held those, but a mass of people stood outside in the churchyard and sang the hymns, until the whole scattered village and the wide fields and the deep woods were filled with the sound of decent folk saying — and singing — goodbye to a friend.

It came for Sir Eustace to say a piece about Joe; parson led him

to the foot of the pulpit, and Sir Eustace went up the five stairs.
He didn't know it, but by the time he'd finished his few words
we knew that there was no one else in the whole world who could
have expressed our feelings half as well. I can't remember a lot of
what he said, but I knew that he kept it simple; it didn't need
anyone to tell me that he meant it:

. . . Joseph Seckley was beloved of this community not only
for his country skills, but because of the breadth of his mind
and the humanity of his judgements. Though now he is gone
from our midst, his fond memory will endure in the hearts of
those who knew and loved him, of those who know, truly, that
they are their brother's keeper . . .

To the graveside then. Bill Figgis, in his best uniform,
managed the crowd with simple requests and pointing finger.

On Joe's coffin they laid his favourite and very expensive gun,
and Chris Butterworth, Henry Wattis and four others young and
strong carried the coffin. Then came more words from the parson,
but I think that each one of us, in our hearts, was praying as well as
the parson could. Me, I was praying, I think, a prayer that real
craftsmanship and real, great people like Joe Seckley should never
vanish from this earth. I knew the manner of man that Joe was in a
way that most present on that day didn't. I had seen his toolshed,
and hanging on the walls, neat, cleaned and greased were every
kind of implement of husbandry, sharp and ready for use.

'Joe, if some on 'em got to know about the tools you have here,
you'd have burglars, it's a treasure house.'

'Wouldn't worry me, Frank. Who steals my purse steals
trash.'

'My Lord,' Evelyn said, 'what a day to go. What a day.' She looked up at the steeple, grey, strong, enduring. 'Swallows are back again. We never know when they die, do we? It always seems the same swallows.'

The coffin was ready for lowering. Young Orb took the gun off. They lowered it, and some walked by to cast a little earth. There's a good, simple headstone at the grave now, but we remember Joe and that's a better memorial. For many months after, as I passed the church which was in sight of Joe's cottage, I thought of all that craftsman's pride hanging in his toolshed, sharp and greased and done right, and waiting. And I thought of Edith Seckley, sitting with folded hands, and Joe in his grave.

CHAPTER SIXTEEN

God Rest Ye Merry Gentlemen

At the back end of 1938 there were many farms where the insensible tractor was still second to the horse, and rightly. It was Christmas time. The children were just nippers, then, with Georgina and Horace going to school, Joyce not quite old enough to go to school, and Archie – well, he was just a distant thought at that time. Georgina and Horace used to walk teo miles twice a day to school. Then they closed it, added a few pieces on to another school about a mile further on, so the children had to walk further.

I must say a bit about this school reorganization, because its echoes sometimes call across the flat lands of our part of the country, and there is a man whose name is remembered. It's a Christmas story that started at the beginning of September, maybe even earlier. This was when Mr Sharpe arrived to be headmaster of the school attended by all the marsh children. That would make three classes in all, the headmaster taking the older ones, dear old Mrs Lubbock taking the tinies, and a girl named Jane Stewart, from Spalding, looked after the middle class.

I first heard of him when my employer was on the school board of management. 'Appointed a new headmaster for the school, Frank.'

'That's good,' I said, 'Is he a firm sort of feller?'

My employer's eyes twinkled. 'Oh yes, I think you can say that. He was an assistant head of a school in Stepney.'

'Ah,' I said, 'and we've got one or two round here what could do with a firm hand, haven't we?'

I heard later that a small group of our local 'heavies' met Mr Sharpe before school started. There was young Tom Hartford (later killed in Palestine), Griff Lewis's boy and one or two more who were lounging about at the playground gate, some sitting on the pillars, others sort of recumbent on the wall. So, this was where they got their first glimpse.

Mr Sharpe was short and thick-set, looking a bit like the bole of an oak; he had a thinning thatch of black hair, and round, gold-rimmed spectacles. He was carrying two heavy suitcases. As for the bright lads, they'd met schoolmasters before, and they knew how to appear unimpressed.

Mr Sharpe stopped at the cluttered gate and spoke quietly. 'I would like to come through, please.'

Now, if they'd had any sense, they'd have realized that this was not the time for an exhibition of fancy bad manners. Something should have told them.

The Lewis boy made the first speech, and short it was. 'We usually hop over the wall.'

Mr Sharpe stood quite still in the drowsy September sun

holding his suitcases. 'Open the gate for me, please,' he said. 'I wish to put these cases of books into the school.'

'Carry on,' Tom Hartford said airily.

'No business of ours,' another lad said.

There was a short flurry which involved all the boys, both suitcases, and Mr Sharpe. When the smoke of battle cleared, Mr Sharpe was holding the arms of Hartford and Lewis as in a vice. 'Now,' he said, 'I wish to go through that gate in a proper manner. Open it, and have the goodness to carry these two cases for me.'

They did as they were told, just hoping that no one saw them.

One evening in late September when I came home, I found Horace in a no-talking mood.

'What did you do at school, boy?'

Grunt.

'Did you get the cane?'

Negative double grunt.

'You going to be in the football team this season?'

Small burbling noise.

I saw that here was a brick wall I needn't bother to push against, so I went outside and found Georgina, who was skipping with some other nippers.

'What's up with our Horace?' I asked.

My daughter and her mates giggled. Georgina volunteered the information. 'Mr Sharpe told him off, and Horace didn't know what he meant.'

'Talk in Russian, did he?'

'No, but when we were coming in from play Horace shoved his way in front of us, and Mr Sharpe told him that this was bad manners.'

Evelyn came up to us. 'Hear that?' I asked.

'My word, I did. It'll be a real change for some of them to mind their manners. Ladies first. Now that's something that's supposed to be going out of fashion.'

In the following few weeks, we learned that quite a lot of Mr Sharpe's ideas were out of fashion, and most of 'em everybody over thirty at least would like to have seen become law. Other aspects of his life were also noted: he had someone to dust and clean for him; he was a good cook, a good fisherman and a holy terror to any child under his care who dared to disobey. And there were some there who weren't very good at obeying. But they were to learn.

Uproar number one came with the beating given by Mr Sharpe, in the eyes of the whole school, to two bright sparks: both wanted to have their teas standing up. Their fathers asked questions, and surveyed the reddish lashes on the backsides of their sons, and went to see Mr Sharpe.

Mr Sharpe came to meet them with a smile of welcome. They first asked roughly, 'I want to know why you hurt my boy. He said he wasn't doing nothing wrong.'

'I'd like to know what mine did, too,' said the other.

Mr Sharpe told them in no uncertain terms what he thought they'd done wrong. 'It would be perfectly within the bounds of possibility,' he continued 'for both your boys to land up in court on a charge which, I believe, is known as G.B.H.' He glanced sternly at one and then the other. 'Do I look like a man who would cane a boy for nothing? Do I? Would you gentlemen like to see the punishment book, so that you know it is correctly entered?'

Punishment book. They didn't know there was such a thing. But Mr Sharpe showed them.

'Bullying? Six strokes? Nobody could make a mess of a boy's backside in six strokes the way you did my son!'

'I can,' said Mr Sharpe, taking back the book and closing it with a snap. 'I did, and, if necessary, I shall repeat the performance.'

'If you touch my boy —'

'Your boy is a coward, an idler, a bad influence, a teller of dirty jokes and a twister of little boys' arms until they give him some of their sweets. But, I assure you that I am going to do my duty by your boy, no matter how painful it may be for both of us. If Miss Stewart hadn't been very quick, your boys might well have been the cause of two little boys losing their eyesight.'

That made them think.

'What'd they do?'

'Two little boys were putting out some powder colour for a painting lesson. These two boys of yours came into the classroom, threw the powder about, and some got into the little boys' eyes. Miss Stewart found them crying, and she washed their eyes and kept on washing until they could open their eyes. Then she washed again and again, until their eyes left off smarting.

'So,' said Mr Sharpe, 'if you two gentlemen like to take your badly treated sons to see Doctor Jarvis this evening, you will no doubt find the parents of the little victims there too. I rather think you'll have some difficulty in convincing *them* that it was just a boyish prank.'

I never knew, until I'd met Mr Sharpe, and heard of his actions and opinions, that a man could be so right and so disliked. The point I missed was that people hated his guts because he *was* right, and kept on being so. He was a highly educated man who expected reasons and facts, and anyone who couldn't meet him on his level, well, they were left open-mouthed and staring.

To begin with, there was the matter of absences. It had been understood (or ignored) that there were times when all hands, strong schoolboys and girls as well, were needed on the farm. But it wasn't in the regulations, and Mr Sharpe had copies of the regulations sent to every parent.

But uproars breed uproars, like the way a damp jumping jack can suddenly start cracking again. Jack Lake's middle son, Ted, had been away from school, and he brought Mr Sharpe a note. Having done this, the lad joined his class as they marched into assembly. Mr Sharpe called him back. He held the note, a folded-over rumpled bit of paper, between finger and thumb. 'Edward, what do you call this?'

'A note sir.'

Mr Sharpe had a thousand-watt glare which could bring total silence. It did so now. 'I am a headmaster, and I accept notes written on decent paper and in ink, with a correctly addressed envelope. I do not accept any old scrap of paper. Take this note back to your parents,' he said to the petrified Teddy Lake, 'and tell them what I have said. You may *all* of you tell your parents what I have just said.'

They told their parents all right, and the district buzzed about 'that there new headmaster'.

The next uproar ensued when Sharpey was invited to meet Miss Dowling, who had once admitted to me that she had seen fifty summers. Sharpey listened to 'her choir' as she called it, which went round singing carols. She loved the sweet natural singing of the children, so she said. But she did something which she shouldn't have; she asked Mr Sharpe what he thought, not knowing that Mr Sharpe always gave an opinion when asked for it.

'They sing out of tune,' Mr Sharpe said, 'because singing in tune is not a natural thing; it has to be taught. Their vowels are

terrible, their phrasing slovenly, and I wouldn't, in their present
state of incompetence, have them offer up to the Lord *His* tunes.
If this were done, I would fear that they might all be struck by a
bolt from heaven.'

He walked out, just in time to miss hearing Miss Dowling's
tears.

It was not much later that Mr Sharpe announced that the *school*
choir this Christmas would be the official carol singers for the
area. Door-to-door begging was forbidden, and, in his opinion,
only under his charge would there be a choir sufficiently well
trained to sing carols 'with the requisite sweetness and reverence'.
And when the village (including my missis) was fizzing with
annoyance at this, Mr Sharpe had it spread abroad that he was an
FRCO, if anyone doubted his musical ability.

It was a frosty night, and clear, when Georgina and Horace went
out for their first night as members of the *official* choir, touring
round the district and singing carols. On Christmas Eve they
were to sing around the model manger in the church. Which
reminds me – they were a couple of lambs short, so Sharpey
carved them out of pine and then coloured them.

So, it was the week before Christmas, 1938. Our part of the
country was making all preparations; what I mean is, they were
busy with the commercial side of it, and I can't tell how they
went on with the more important side of it, the feast of Christ.

There wasn't quite the conveyor belt system in operation as
there is these days. Three or four farms would join together and
round up the necessary labour for plucking and drawing and
generally getting the birds ready for the oven. The down feathers
used to be picked separately. But not all slaughterings were

official. There was many a pig among our scattered community who woke up, as you might say, with a knife in his throat and a bowl catching the blood; only thing wasted was the squeal.

Under my guidance, there was food and water and hay and straw for all living things on the farm. This was the 'over Christmas' system, but the truth of it was that the animals weren't left on their own for many hours over the twenty-four. It was always a good idea to walk round and see how the animals were faring. Never let them feel that man has deserted them. Of them all, the horse is least likely to misbehave; as I may have said before, the horse has sense.

When I came in to tea, Georgina said, 'Mr Sharpe went away this afternoon.' She'd already told her mother, and now wanted to tell me. Horace would have liked to do that, but he had his mouth full.

Eventually, however, he was able to say, 'He had to go to London.'

Evelyn said, 'Frank, I shall have to have some more holly; place looks nothing when you have to skimp on green stuff and holly.'

'I'll find some,' I said, and turned my attention to Georgina and Horace. 'Who's been taking top class today, then?'

'Mr Tasker, and he wasn't wearing his dog collar.'

'Who's doing the rounds with the choir, then?'

'Mr Tasker and Miss Dowling.'

I reflected that Sharpey might be being tactful, getting these two to work with the choir after he'd shown them both they knew nothing about choir training. Season of peace and good will, I suppose.

'I should hope so too,' Evelyn said. 'They can't go round without a man in charge.'

It was a dry night, very cold, very clear, with snow deep in the ditches where the snowploughs had thrust it. I was walking home, crunching at each step, checking over again in my mind if there'd been anything that was missed, anything which would cause the stock trouble. Then, taking the walk steady and leaning forward a bit, I started to think about January. I must be an optimist; I don't think of us being done with summer until the first week in November, and as soon as Christmas and New Year have come and gone, I start to think of spring.

So I was walking home and quite enjoying it, even though I'd done a hard day's work. Then came the sound of children singing, carrying across the steely countryside with great sweetness. Real sweetness this year, and all because of Sharpey. That choir sounded so good I reckon the one at King's College, Cambridge would have had a bit of competition from our kids.

I realized, as I drew nearer to the singing, that they were near the cross-roads, not fifty yards from our house; I realized too that this was probably their last performance, except for the church services. Now I could see them, standing in a circle, with Mr Sharpe conducting and a light on a pole being held by somebody else. And then the thing which I thought was real lovely; the people from the nearby houses were out and singing with them. I arrived just as they'd finished 'Oh come, all ye faithful', and people clapped and a little lad with a red nose and five yards of muffler to match was going round collecting.

Horace and Georgina came to me when the singing was done; Mr Sharpe came with them. 'Ah, just the man I want to see. No time like the present, Mr Moore. Must look ahead. . . .' He broke off to say goodbyes and thank-yous to the dispersing choir. 'I'm thinking about Easter.'

'Ain't got Christmas done yet,' I said, 'you must like work, Mr Sharpe. What can I do for you?'

Evelyn appeared out of the dark. 'Don't stand there and get

cold,' she said, 'come into our house and warm yourselves. Horace and Georgina, in you go at once.'

So Mr Sharpe walked with us to our house. 'I want a donkey,' he said. 'A good quiet one for the Easter pageant.'

'Ah, Mr Tasker asked you did he?'

Sharpey chuckled. 'He doesn't know, yet. But he will. And we shall have one.'

'Well,' I said, 'I'll ask around. Not common in these parts, donkeys.'

We walked up our path, and missis let us in front way. As we went in, he turned to the man with the lamp. 'You too, Thomas.' He waited, and his voice became stern. 'Thomas, I told you; you're wanted. Come inside.'

So the man came in.

'Tadge!' I exclaimed. Tadge it was, but Tadge clean, shaved and hair cut, wearing second-hand but good and serviceable clothes and boots.

'Hello, Mr Moore,' he said.

'His real name,' Sharpey said, 'is Thomas Elvin Wykeham. He is now a good working man, and a necessary member of our community.'

'Amen to that,' the vicar said, and so we all had a drink and thought about this transformation. The vicar stayed for a little, after Tadge — I mean Tom — had gone. The vicar's none-too-frequent smile was in evidence. 'Mr Sharpe found him sleeping in the old toolshed. He took him indoors, stripped him, washed him and cut his hair, gave him some clothes to wear and a bed to sleep in.'

'Barking out orders like the sergeant-major on parade.'

'Probably, Mr Moore. That's the way he does things. But he is a true Christian, and I must try to get on with him. It is plainly

my duty to do that. He says that Tom is now the school caretaker, and is paying him accordingly.'

'But wouldn't it take a full meeting of the school board to approve that?' I asked.

The vicar tried to stop smiling, but didn't succeed. 'I have an idea that Mr Sharpe will be at that meeting, and I imagine that his caretaker will be accepted.'

'I reckon he will,' I said. 'In fact, I'd bet on it.'

When the vicar had gone, Evelyn said, 'What do you think of all that, then?'

I thought of our kids, snug in bed, I thought of the farm animals, snug and warm and well-fed, and then I realized that, whatever we had done for Tadge it had been no more than patronage. I said that to Evelyn, and she was in full agreement.

'It's taken a stranger,' I said, 'and a none too popular one at that, to show us up by real deeds, not words. Vicar's right; Sharpey is a Christian gentleman.'

'He is. And I think, Frank, that it'll be the beginning of a change in him. After all, everybody in these parts who's under fifteen lives in terror of him.'

'The fear of God, I reckon,' I said. 'The old flaming sword idea.'

'That's what I mean,' Evelyn said.

She couldn't have been more wrong. The day the kids got back to school, three big lads got thrashed for ramming snow down girls' necks, and another two were walloped for watering and resurfacing a slide.

And Sharpey? No, of course he didn't. Sharpey didn't change, how could he? He was true to himself; what more do you want?